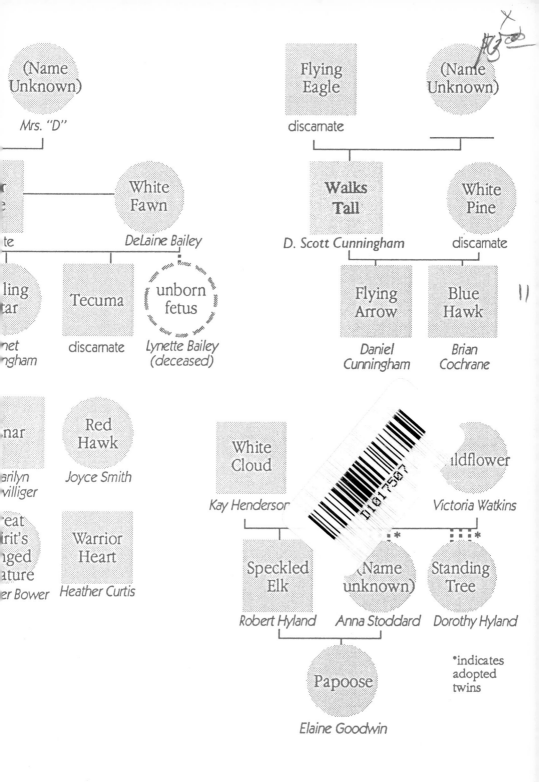

Graphic Art by Randy Mishler

A Tribe Returned

Books by Janet Cunningham

Inner Selves: The Feminine* Path to Weight Loss
(*for men and women who value their intuitive nature)

Co-authored with Michael Ranucci

Caution: Soul Mate Ahead!

Breakthroughs
to the
Unconscious

A Tribe Returned

JANET CUNNINGHAM

DEEP FOREST PRESS

Second Edition 1994

Published in the United States by

Deep Forest Press
P.O. Drawer 4
Crest Park, CA 92326

Cover art and Illustrations: Orazio J. Salati
Jacket design: Kasey Fancett
Photo by: Heather D'Amore

Library of Congress No. 94-72318
ISBN 1-882530-09-8

Printed by Jostens, Visalia, CA

To

E. Scott Cunningham

who started our memories

and

To

The Tribe

That Has Returned

Acknowledgments

My sincere appreciation goes to each person portrayed in this story.

I especially want to acknowledge the support of my family—Scottie, Daniel, and E. Scott Cunningham, Sara and Jennifer Bower, and Ginger Bower Zack. Your faith in me and my work has always been something that I could count on, when I began to question everything else.

Marda Hanford, DeLaine Bailey, Deb Nelsen, Karen Kim, and Kate Paul were a constant source of motivation in their belief that this story must be told. You gave me courage when I may have faltered.

Michael Ranucci and Orazio (Roz) Salati fueled me with their enthusiasm, push, and loving friendship. It is through your nurturing energy that this book is completed.

Thank you to Jim and Jenny Johnson for support and sharing the vision that this is a story that needs to be shared.

Thank you to Joanne Garland, copy editor, for her outstanding professional contribution. In addition, Joanne, the sincerity of your understanding and appreciation of our story has been heartfelt.

And my deepest gratitude to Winafred Lucas, Ph.D., editor, for her demanding professionalism in the publication of this book. Winafred, I appreciate the months of time, energy, wisdom, and loving attention you have given to this project. Your encouragement and recognition of my work has strengthened me.

Table of Contents

List of Illustrations

Foreword

Reincarnation as a belief system has captured the attention of the great minds of all time and through the centuries hundreds of books have been written about it. However, few have dealt with groups of people returning together. *A Tribe Returned* is a remarkable exposition of souls reincarnating to be together in another physical experience.

This book is more than a gripping saga of a people persecuted by the intruding white race and driven from their ancestral lands. It is a moving delineation of the spiritual philosophy of a people steeped in ancient traditions. From the opening chapter to the final dramatic ending the reader is drawn into an empathic encounter with these beautiful Indian people.

As the tale unfolds one wonders why a group of people so spiritually oriented and in harmony with their environment should suffer such barbarous annihilation, but history is replete with similar catastrophic events, among them the trials of the Essenes in ancient times. One can only assume that if spiritual evolution is the purpose of life on this planet, then every soul must experience the discordant as well as the beautiful. The long road from hate and rage to love and acceptance must necessarily include expressions of man's dark side. Convincing evidence supports the theory that all physical experiences are lessons for growth, and the important aspect of all experiences is what we do about them and how we change and grow spiritually as a result.

A Tribe Returned is a powerful witness to the validity of this philosophy. This tribe, already steeped in integrity and spiritual values, suffered physical indignities, yet returned in the present life to continue as loving and caring people rather than as individuals seeking revenge for past injustices. What a tribute this book is to those in the tribe who in their current lives demonstrate this kind of spiritual power!

While reading this book the reader is struck by the insensitivity of the white intruders. This does not imply that all Indians were as evolved as the Oglalas, or that all invaders were cruel butchers, but history has produced many accounts of injustices and cruelty perpetrated by white soldiers, and there is strong evidence that most Indians were friendly until they were taken advantage of and their lands confiscated.

A Tribe Returned is a sensitive but dramatic account of one tribe that epitomized the Indian philosophy at its best with all the attributes of a people in harmony with their universe. Regression therapists will find fascinating case studies in the extensive past-life descriptions of the primary Indian personalities. Approximately 25 individuals were included in the study, with considerable detail focused on the chief and his daughter. Much of the tribe's philosophy is revealed through the conversations between these two.

However, the real value for the therapist, particularly one involved in past-life regression therapy, lies in an analysis of the individuals in their current lives. The individuals in the group, almost without exception, are experiencing a variety of personality and emotional situations and conflicts similar to those experienced in the tribe. Some of these exhibit remarkable parallels to their past-life episodes and characteristics.

While working in altered states in their current lifetime the group discovered that the chief was still carrying a pervasive sense of guilt because he believed his wrong decision had resulted in the massacre of his tribe. The group worked in meditation for his release and felt they had succeeded in bringing their chief to a state of peace.

A Tribe Returned is a remarkable true life saga that keeps the reader emotionally involved between sadness and anger right up to the final page. Janet Cunningham has made a significant contribution both to our knowledge of Indian history and to our understanding of past-life regression therapy.

Hazel M. Denning, Ph.D.
Co-Founder and Past President,
Association for Past-Life Research and Therapies

Preface

Is it a true story? Did the tribe really exist? Is it imagination? Could over 25 people be participating in the same fantasy? Did this group of people agree to come back together? Are all the past-life regressions that I have done and the unconscious memories from such a diversified group of people real? And if the memories and emotions are not real, where do they come from? Could they be archetypes of the Collective Unconscious—or aspects of our soul energy?

This is my story, and I still have difficulty believing that it all happened. I have difficulty accepting, while I live as Janet Cunningham, the "coincidences" related to this experience. My story includes the events and memories of clients, friends, and family. Most of them were much more accepting than I was of a Native American incarnation together. Did I simply want to avoid facing it as truth, to avoid my own personal memories? I did not know if I would be strong enough to re-live this past incarnation as it had been uncovered by others. I knew the emotion that would arise in me as I participated in and watched others go through the memories of re-living that lifetime. And—I am the hypnotherapist. Until February 1991 I did not have anyone else who could guide me through that particular regression in the way that I needed to experience it.

The story is true. I have written it as developments actually happened in my life. The only changes that have been made are the names and descriptions of nine people for their privacy; these names have been changed at their request. In these instances, any similarity to persons living or dead is purely coincidental.

All other names, people, situations, and experiences are real and written as they occurred in my life. I take full responsibility for my perceptions related to them.

As this story is told, each person stands in courage and strength, saying, "This is who I am." The powerlessness that results from unconscious memories from the past is released as each person stands in *power and love*, saying, "This is who I am."

I give my thanks to all of you...
- for the experiences you brought to me.
- for the push to my own healing.
- for the love re-connected.

*This is not a story about reincarnation:
It is a story about love.*

Janet Cunningham

Members of the Tribe

(In the order of their appearance)

Janet Cunningham (Falling Star) - Hypnotherapist whose clients and friends began to retrieve memories of a Native American past lifetime.

E. Scott Cunningham (Silver Cloud) - Janet's husband, Scott, who as an anniversary gift to his wife commissioned a painting of an Indian chief whom he and others recognized as Silver Eagle.

Mrs. D. - An elderly woman who painted the portrait of Silver Eagle. One channeled message referred to her as Silver Eagle's mother in the Indian lifetime.

Sara Bower - The wife of Janet's brother in this life. With her developing psychic abilities she was able see herself in the Indian lifetime as Silver Eagle's older sister.

DeLaine Bailey (White Fawn) - A dairy farmer's wife, former co-worker of Janet and now an intuitive massage therapist. DeLaine recognized herself as Silver Eagle's mate.

Marda Hanford (Little Feather) - A secretary who once worked for Janet and who finally uncovered her own tragic death in the Indian tribe.

Deb Nelson (Flaming Arrow) - A longtime follower of Native American traditions and teachings. Her regression uncovered a tribal life where she was a powerful warrior who wanted to fight for the land.

Dorothy (Dot) Hyland* (Standing Tree) - A client who saw herself as an apprentice to a medicine woman and who chose to go to a cave and die rather than "eat the white man's poison."

Joyce Smith (Red Hawk) - An astrologer who recovered memories of being an old man who went with others to a cave to die.

Victoria (Vickie) Watkins* (Wildflower) - Dot Hyland's younger sister who recognized herself in the Indian lifetime as a confused and forgetful old woman.

Robert Hyland* (Speckled Elk) - Dot Hyland's husband who retrieved memories of training to become a medicine man and of leading a small group of tribe members to a cave to die.

Anna Stoddard* - A friend of Robert Hyland. From the beginning her presence felt threatening to Robert's wife, Dot. This became understood when memories were recovered that Robert had fathered Anna's child in the Indian lifetime.

Elaine Goodwin* (papoose) - A petite businesswoman who saw herself as the child in the tribe born to Robert and Anna. She was taken by a soldier after her mother had been killed but refused food and died.

Margaret Osborne* (Rising Sun) - Friend of Sara Bower who recognized her as Silver Eagle's second mate.

Marilyn Terwilliger* (Enar) - A client who sought help with painful childhood memories. Dot soon recognized Marilyn as the tribal medicine woman under whom she had studied.

Orazio (Roz) Salati (Golden Winged Hawk) - An artist and art teacher who taught pottery and weaving using Native American themes. After unblocking his creativity he began to produce massive paintings that depicted the massacre of the tribe where he had been the mother of Running Deer. He died before the massacre and helped the souls of those killed to make their transition.

Kate Paul (Little Star) - A former nun who had worked on a Sioux reservation in North Dakota. She left the convent after 28 years. Shortly afterwards she underwent a regression and saw herself as Marda's sister in the tribe.

Michael Ranucci (Running Deer) - Close friend of Roz and Kate. His own regression uncovered an Indian lifetime as the son of Roz (Golden Winged Hawk). He witnessed the massacre before being decapitated.

D. Scott (Scottie) Cunningham* (Walks Tall) - Janet's other son who became angry when he first saw the painting of Silver Eagle. In the tribe he was a warrior.

Karen Kim (Little Blue Mountain) - Owner of a fine arts and craft gallery stocked with quality Native American art and jewelry. Her tribal memories proved too painful to be seen clearly, but Sara saw Karen being tortured by fire.

Daniel (Dan) Cunningham (Flying Arrow) - Janet's son, whose meditations revealed tribal memories of being an Indian scout in communication with the spirit of a hawk.

Heather Curtis (Warrior Heart) - A former student of Roz, now living in Florida. Her regression uncovered an Indian lifetime as a strong warrior who was killed during the massacre by being dragged by the neck behind a wagon.

Timothy Gardner* (White Owl) - Marda's nephew. He encouraged Chief Silver Eagle to fight the white man but during that fight took his own life with an arrow.

Lynette Bailey (fetus) - DeLaine's oldest daughter who took her own life at age 19. In the Indian life Lynette had been DeLaine's unborn child at the time of the massacre.

Judy DeGuzman (Whispering Dove) - An acquaintance of Kate, whom Kate recognized as the Indian woman who had been her mother and who had died giving birth to Marda.

Brian Cochrane (Blue Hawk) - A current friend of Dan Cunningham and recognized by Sara as Dan's brother and Scottie's son in the tribe.

Kay Henderson (White Cloud) - A friend who was recognized by Dot and Robert as a medicine man in the tribe.

Ginger Zack (papoose) - Sara's daughter, seen as Karen Kim's infant child in the tribe.

Jennifer Bower (Great Spirit's Winged Creature) - Sara's other daughter, seen as not an Indian but as a person of spirit energy who assisted the tribe.

Claire (White Pine) - Spirit energy channeled by Sara and sensed by Scottie. In the tribal lifetime she had been Scottie's mate.

Tecuma - Spirit energy, who had been Silver Eagle's son and Falling Star's (Janet's) younger brother.

Silver Eagle - Chief of a small Oglala tribe in the Dakotas. After witnessing the torturous death of each member of his tribe, Silver Eagle locked himself away in darkness in a self-imposed exile. He blamed himself for not heeding his visions that the land would pass away from his people and that the white faces would become chiefs. Today members of the tribe occasionally feel his presence or receive messages from him related to the continued healing and integrity of the tribe.

* Pseudonyms

Silver Eagle by Mrs. D.

Chapter I

Silver Eagle

In the summer of 1986, a year before our 25th wedding anniversary, my husband Scott planned a special gift for me for the occasion. Knowing that I used Indian guides for inner meditation work, he asked an artist friend, Mrs. D. as she was called, then in her late eighties, to paint a portrait of an Indian. Though well-known for her landscapes, Mrs. D. seldom painted portraits but she agreed to Scott's request. The only suggestion Scott made about the painting was, "Paint it from your mind's eye."

It was unusual for Scott to plan such a thing, especially so far ahead of our anniversary. In the beginning he meant the painting to be a surprise, but he grew too excited to keep it secret. When he told me about his commission I coaxed him to share more about it, but he had little to tell because his instruction had been minimal. I looked forward with curiosity to the picture's arrival. Would it look like one of my Indian guides whom my psychic sister-in-law Sara could see? Would it be male or female? Young or mature? Warrior or chief?

On the day that the painting arrived that fall, I was alone. I decided to open my present right then rather than when Scott came home, just in case he tried to make me wait until our anniversary. But as I carried the cumbersome box into the dining room and laid it on the table I felt a sudden uneasiness and apprehension. I had expected excitement—but what was this strange feeling?

I opened the box and saw a painting of an Indian chief. I liked what I saw, and yet the chief's face looked sad and full of pain, and as I stared into this face I felt uncomfortable. When Scott arrived home I showed him the painting, but to avoid making him feel that I didn't appreciate it, I did not mention my discomfort. Instead I said rather flippantly, "Let's give him a name. What do you think his name is?"

Scott responded immediately, "His name is Silver Eagle."

The certainty with which he replied surprised me. "Do you think that is what we should call him, or are you saying that is what you think his name is?"

Scott could not explain other than to say, "That's the name that came to me. His name is Silver Eagle."

I felt eager to show the painting to my brother's wife, Sara, when she arrived from Maryland three days later.

Sara has a conservative and practical nature, perhaps from growing up in the farmlands of Missouri. Even her dress that day was conservative; she wore a trim hand-quilted jacket over her red polyester blouse and black slacks. Short brown hair framed her porcelain-like complexion and natural pink blush on her cheeks. Sara belonged to a weekly quilting group. Despite her conservative orientation, she found that the calming action of quilting helped her to move into altered states. While in such a state she could see a person's spirit guides and relay what these guides communicated. Over the years we had stretched our intuitive boundaries together, and I had grown to trust and respect her psychic abilities.

We crossed to the office wing of my spacious old Victorian home and sat comfortably in what I called the "hypnosis room." The carpeted floor and the paneling and shake shingles across one wall made this room cozy and less like an office. A hanging plant and the scent of wood added to the relaxed atmosphere.

Sara gazed at the painting. She sank into an altered state and began to speak slowly and softly:

> *Many, many years ago upon the plains of this our country we were a strong nation.... There is such pain...it's very painful. I have not shared with another soul my pain. It is my burden to carry throughout all time. This I do according to Indian custom. I will never walk again upon my beloved land because of what*

I have done. Because of me, my people suffered and died. It is difficult to go on.... Please, I must wait until I can compose myself.... (Long pause.)

I had a daughter, a gift from Great Spirit, one chosen to lead my people, but because of me they all died. I thought that we could win. Our battle was a struggle to hang onto our precious land. Because of me they perished. I carry the pain within my heart. I cannot walk the precious land ever again.

My woman, my mate, was extremely fair. How I loved her! And how I loved our daughter! And how I loved my people! My vision spoke to me and said that my land would pass away from me and the white faces would become chiefs.

I vowed this would never happen. Many times I spoke at council, urging my brave young warriors to stand and fight for our beloved land. They agreed, but later when we fought we were outnumbered and beaten. Then after we had lost many warriors, we were attacked in the middle of the night. Many of our women and children were murdered by the cavalry, but I was able to protect my mate, my woman and my daughter.

Some other members of the tribe also survived. I led our small party of survivors deep into the nearby forest. I promised all survivors that our land would once again be returned to us, but alas, we were tracked down by the cavalry. Because I was chief, my mate, my woman, and my beautiful daughter were strung up, bound hand and foot, drawn and quartered.

Tears began to run down my face. Was the chief talking about me?

The pain was too much to bear. I reached for my knife. I, also, was strung up but not put to death until each of the survivors was strung up, drawn and quartered. It is because of me that my people lost their land. Those people died whom I loved dearly. I did not heed my visions. I truly believed that we were a more powerful people and that our land would remain our land. I am ashamed for what I have done and I've locked myself away in time and space and have not been able ever to share my story with another soul.

My mother painted this picture. Only through her would I come. She has silly woman ideas about forgiveness and new starts. I felt that she was wrong, but she insisted upon bringing me forward to my daughter.

Through the talent of my mother I now see my fair daughter once more. What joy it brings to my heart, for I thought it not possible that she would survive our death. It is difficult for me to talk now. I am confused but full of joy to see my daughter alive and living on our precious land once more. I still carry my shame within my heart.

I know this image on canvas is a gift for a special occasion in my daughter's life. I am not worthy to be here. I wish you to burn this picture.

Sara grew overwhelmed by emotion. I hung onto my logic, wondering *Is this possible? Can this be real? Daughter?*

I grasped at something for possible confirmation before she lost the contact. "What is my father's name?" I asked, aware that Sara did not know the name given by Scott.

The words fell out of her mouth, "My name is Silver Eagle."

Chapter II

The Beginning: 1973-1982

Where did it all start? From the early seventies we were drawn to meet, a small group of women in the southern part of upstate New York who shared a past that in the beginning we were not aware that we had had. Gradually others joined to share mutual experiences. Those who learned over the years that they had lived in the Indian lifetime began their current lives in West Virginia, Missouri, Maryland, Pennsylvania, Massachusetts, New York, England, Canada, and Italy. We came together without knowing why we came and found the emerging shared scenario to be a deep surprise.

We began to contact one another during the years before I became involved in regression therapy. At that time none of us had any knowledge of a past lifetime that we had shared. However, prior to our meeting several of the group had already been drawn to connections with an unknown Indian past, though at the time we did not understand the significance of these connections.

One had worked on a Sioux Indian reservation in North Dakota for three years. A married couple had elected over the years to give to only one charity, a Sioux mission in South Dakota. One member had owned a boutique that specialized in quality Native American art while another had participated in Native American rituals and teachings. One of the group had woven and potted using Indian art and techniques and had taught these skills to others.

I had done none of these things. In fact, I had only two connections with Native American culture: a sense of siding with the

Indians when I saw cowboy and Indian movies and a special Indian Halloween costume.

The costume was one I wore on Halloween during my elementary school days for a party and a parade. My mother enjoyed making costumes for my sister and me and often sewed elaborate outfits that ranged from Porky Pig or Bugs Bunny with huge ears and fluffy tail to a beautiful lady in a feminine ruffled dress. However, during the six years of my elementary school days my favorite was an Indian costume made from a tan buckskin-like fabric sewed into pants and overshirt with fringe on the bottom and long sleeves. My mother made a band for my head and among her jewelry I found some beads to put around my neck. She braided my long brown hair into pigtails and I got to wear lipstick! I remember looking in the mirror and thinking that I looked like a beautiful Indian princess. I loved how I looked and felt disappointed that I could wear this costume only one day out of my life.

I grew up in West Virginia where traditional beliefs guided my life and reincarnation was not one of those beliefs. When I look back now I realize how sheltered and protected such a life was, a protection that was continued in my relationship with my husband, Scott, whom I met in 1955 and married in 1962.

Scott, unlike me, had always believed in reincarnation and I became open to its possibility, though the subject of earlier lives was not important to me then. Though over the years reincarnation actually made sense despite my traditional Protestant upbringing, I hadn't yet recovered the sort of personal experience of a prior lifetime that had proven so convincing to Scott. Without a personal experience the topic of past lives seldom came up and I happily gave birth to two sons and busied myself being a wife and mother, my goal during those years. Several moves kept life interesting and exciting. Scott was a good husband and father, and both of us, being solidly grounded in this life, had little impetus to explore the possibility of other lifetimes.

DeLaine

In 1973 we moved to the southern part of New York State, where for several years I worked for a nationally known weight-control organization. There I met DeLaine Bailey, a fellow instructor for our organization. After my husband, DeLaine was the first of the tribe to emerge, though of course I did not know anything about this at the time and our awareness of ancient ties evolved only gradually in the years to come.

I phoned DeLaine one day to suggest that we travel together to a business conference. Later she told me that after my call she remarked to her husband, "I don't know about going to the conference with this woman—she sounds like a snooty la-de-da."

When I drove to pick up DeLaine she introduced me to some fifty cows. I had never been on a dairy farm before and marveled that DeLaine had been up since four A.M. working alongside her husband in the barn doing the milking. She hurried through last-minute instructions for the farm and family before she gathered her belongings for our day-long trip.

Farmer and snooty la-de-da hit it off immediately. We talked about our work, families, and lives. We were the same age, close to the same size, and had brown hair that we wore at that time in the same short straight style. When I met one of the company supervisors after our arrival, she said, "Janet, you look like DeLaine! You could be taken for sisters." That comment, so prophetic in terms of later discoveries, would often be heard over the years as we worked together. On a few occasions I changed my hairstyle and was surprised when I saw DeLaine the next time—unknowingly she had made the same hairstyle change and we laughed at the coincidence. Our resemblance was so striking that there were even times when someone stopped me in a grocery store to say hello and ask about the farm and cows. Me with cows? DeLaine laughed heartily at that idea.

DeLaine had four children, and her youngest boy was the same age as mine. Her oldest child, a daughter named Lynette, who was to play a part in our emerging story, was causing her a great deal of stress at the time. Lynette was a lovely girl, outgoing and active, but she and DeLaine always seemed to be at odds. One morning DeLaine's husband phoned me to say that DeLaine would need a substitute instructor for her classes. In the calm voice that is typical of someone in shock he said simply, "Lynette is dead." She had been found in bed by DeLaine's sister, with whom she had been living while attending college. Lynette had been drinking at a party, and no one knew whether the sleeping pills by her bed had been taken intentionally or accidentally.

Marda

The next tribe member emerged shortly after this time when I moved to an administrative position in the company. Marda Hanford, a shy quiet woman, four feet eleven, with glasses and thick brown hair that she wore short with bangs covering much of her face, became my secretary and bookkeeper. She worked with me for several years and could be counted on to be pleasant and congenial. In her work Marda was slow and methodical, and her efficiency with details freed me to concentrate on other aspects of the business and counseling. The contrast between DeLaine's outspoken and outgoing personality with its constant fire and rapid action and Marda's passive, non-assuming, slow and quiet nature was striking, yet they were best friends.

On the whole, our business together moved along in a traditional way, but several incidents propelled me gradually to look beyond conventional awareness. At one monthly staff-meeting an employee, returning from a vacation in the West, gave me an unusual silver charm as a gift. As I thanked her, she dropped the charm into my hand and I saw that it was a tiny, beautifully crafted Indian headdress. *How strange,* I thought. *I don't have anything to do with Indians.* The charm wasn't appropriate for my charm bracelet that held talismans of family events and of my personal history. I appreciated my colleague's thought but put the little silver headdress aside and forgot it.

One incident stirred up much curiosity in the office, the visit of a co-worker to a psychic for a reading in 1982. *I'd never do that,* I thought. But when my co-worker told me what this psychic had related to her, I found the accuracy and explicitness of the reading surprising, especially the facts that this psychic had mentioned regarding me. *How is that possible?* I wondered. *Can a person's mind do that? And if so, how?* I told Scott about her, and his response was to want to have a reading. "You're kidding!" I exclaimed.

So it was Scott who started us on our path of learning more about realms beyond this physical dimension. Later he was invited to attend a psychic awareness class and I went also, not because I believed that I had such ability but because I was curious about how the mind works in psychic perception. After a while Scott dropped the class, but I continued. Later I wondered if he had gone first as my protector to check it out, which was okay—I valued his opinions and felt pleased that I could talk with him about these new ideas.

Sara

It was my sister-in-law Sara, however, with whom I shared most deeply. Sara and I have always been like sisters, and my sister Judy and I, when Sara married our brother, welcomed her into our family with a feeling she had always belonged. So for nearly thirty years Sara and I had shared a friendship that focused on marriage and raising children.

In 1983 when Sara experienced her psychic opening, it was in my presence. Even though I had been attending psychic awareness classes, this time it was *my* sister-in-law who was actually seeing spirit guides and giving messages. My reaction was, *Good God, this could all be real!* For the next several years she and I learned together—about guides and past lives and psychic phenomena. Again and again I watched her introduce strangers to their guides, and I noticed the shocked expression on their faces when Sara told them things that in the space/time world she could not possibly have known.

On one of her working visits Sara told me, after we had meditated together, that she saw her Indian guide drawing a circle in dirt with a twig, as if he were trying to have her remember something. He wanted both of us to remember some teaching from our past.

"I just don't know what he wants me to remember," she said. "He's going to have to find some other way to get through to me." Two days later, after spontaneously walking into a book store, we found the book *The Medicine Wheel* by Sun Bear.

"That's it!" Sara exclaimed excitedly. "That's what he wants me to remember!" Sara delved into reading and learning about Native American culture, enjoying the strong connection she felt with her Indian spirit guide. Although the information was invaluable, she was told, "You are white woman in white society. Live as white woman in white society."

Sara's psychic abilities continued to grow, and together we expanded our understanding. I found it fascinating—nothing in my background or education had ever touched on this new information. While Sara's accuracy amazed me, there were times when her perceptions proved incorrect, and we learned more as we evaluated these errors. We could see how the mind interferes with clarity of inner perception. Like the majority of people, we had assumed that unless someone were one hundred percent accurate, the psychic process was a fraud, and during the next several years we had to broaden our understanding of how intuitive perception works.

During that time of learning, Sara often came to visit me in New York from her home in Maryland. She became acquainted with DeLaine and Marda, and the four of us began a new phase in our friendship and growth. By this time our children were finishing high school or had entered college or otherwise gone off on their own, leaving us free to embark on a new path that we referred to as our spiritual journey.

On several occasions while driving to work I said a prayer asking to be used as a channel for healing. Years later I would remember that prayer and realize that at the time I had no idea what I was asking. It was one of my first realizations that we need to be very careful what we ask for—we may just get it!

Chapter III

Forming the Circle: 1983

In 1983 Marda invited DeLaine and me to join in a meditation circle that would meet weekly at her house, and gradually others joined us. In a dream she received the name for the group—the Circle of Love. She felt drawn to form the Circle because she wished to understand the many unusual things that she heard her friends discuss. Initially she stayed on the periphery of these discussions, though her trust in us and in the messages that came through us eventually let her begin to accept the less traditional spiritual concepts that we voiced.

Sara was not a regular member of our group, but whenever she was in town she joined us and shared the messages that were channeled through her. Soon, even when she was not there, the rest of us began to tune into messages, symbols, and other perceptions of one another. We expanded our concepts of religion and God, and this period became a time of excitement and discovery. After our meditation we often had lunch together because we had much to talk over and share. These weekly get-togethers to talk and meditate became a high point in our lives.

Joyce

The first to join our small group after its beginning, Joyce Smith, had originally been referred to me by one of my clients. Joyce was an astrologer. I had never met an astrologer and when, during our first phone conversation, she asked my birth date and immediately rattled off information about me, I was amazed. *How could she know such things from my birth date?* I wondered. I invited her to meet DeLaine and Marda, and that led to her inclusion in the group.

Joyce was delightful. Tall, with grey hair and light coloring, she was the epitome of femininity. Although she was in her late fifties, we found her youthfulness and curiosity fun and energizing as she gathered our birth information and shared her impressions. Over lunch she talked about the sign under which a person "chooses" to be born. Joyce had studied astrology for ten years without having anyone with whom to discuss her ideas and discoveries, so she found it a joy to be able to talk freely with such a receptive audience. Her days of isolation were over—all of us in the group felt ready and anxious to hear what this knowledgeable woman had to say, and we were happy when she began to meet with us regularly.

In December of 1983 I left my position with the weight control company and the next April opened my own business, specializing in stress reduction, weight control, counseling, and hypnosis. I did some past-life regression work but never advertised it, preferring to keep my business more traditional.

Dot

Another patient in my private practice who appeared to be right for the group was Dorothy (Dot) Hyland, who came for weight loss in May 1985. She was a tall woman in her forties, one hundred pounds overweight. Her short curly dark brown hair encircled a cheery face. We had met previously at a social function through her husband, a banker. Dot's husband knew that I had opened my own weight control clinic and suggested that she contact me to try to deal with the obesity that had burdened her all her life. She followed his recommendation, but before calling me for an appointment she went to a library to read about hypnosis!

When Dot appeared in my office I felt an instant rapport with her. This connection grew until it seemed obvious that she belonged in our group. On her third appointment, after a traditional therapeutic approach that included reprogramming the mind through hypnosis, she said, "Sometimes I wonder if it's my karma to be fat." I breathed a sigh of relief because with this statement she gave me an opening to explore past lives, since these were already a part of her belief system.

"It is possible that unconscious memories of a past-life situation, such as starvation or obesity, could be affecting this life," I told her. My hypothesis sparked her interest in doing a regression to see if we could learn more about her unconscious need for excess body fat, so I relaxed her with a hypnotic induction, suggesting only that she go to the cause of her problem with obesity.

In the regression she found herself a slim, healthy Indian woman with long black hair who was picking herbs and berries for healing remedies. She recognized herself as a medicine woman in a small tribe. When I moved her to a later period in that life she saw herself making a choice to enter a cave and die rather than "eat white man's poison." Her regression was one of the first to tune into what we would later realize was the massacre of the tribe to which we all belonged, but at that time we had no inkling of this.

The regression answered several questions for Dot at a deep level. In her current life, despite being overweight she had an interest in natural foods and took pride in preparing healthful meals of grains, beans, and rice with herb seasoning that reflected her practice as a medicine woman in the earlier life. Her choice to die by starvation in that earlier life could, I felt, account for times of feeling insatiably hungry in her current life. I was satisfied that the information she had recovered from her unconscious mind related primarily to her weight problem and for the moment thought no more about it.

The Circle Expands

At this time Sara wanted our Circle to make a weekend retreat in the Maryland area. She found a location and began to make plans for what she called our first Medicine Wheel gathering. As the retreat began to materialize, my intuition told me that Dot Hyland was supposed to attend. However, because I had just met her as a client, it seemed inappropriate to propose this. My professional image and my intuitive perception battled for a few days, but the image lost and at the next appointment I found myself inviting Dot to join us on the retreat if she felt so inclined.

She called me before the week was over to say that she would come. In order to have her meet DeLaine, Marda, and Joyce, I arranged her next appointment on the same day that our group met for meditation. After our session I brought her with me to the meeting, and it felt as though we had been waiting for her. I had read of Sun Bear's vision of Circles spreading across the globe, Circles that would bring healing to the earth, and I hoped that Dot's inclusion was a token of the spreading of our Circle.

Our trip to Maryland was light, fun, and filled with the kind of minor miracles that we had begun to expect. Dot, especially, could hardly believe that she was with us—it was the first time she had done something like this without her husband, Robert. This was also DeLaine's first vacation without her family. With her accustomed competence in managing, she took charge of food preparation, scheduling, and finances, and the rest of us let her take over with no objections.

When Sara and Dot met at the retreat, it was as though old friends had been reunited after a lifetime apart. During the retreat Sara introduced Dot to spiritual guides, and once again I was amazed. Sara had never met Dot, had little information about her, and yet began to channel what Dot's guides were saying, a process that always touched the soul. Sara accessed a reality that I could not understand but could not deny.

Margaret Osborne, a friend of Sara's who lived in Maryland, also attended the retreat. Margaret and DeLaine hit it off at once, and took turns sharing tips on the massage and foot reflexology that they had both begun to learn. At that time Margaret had not thought much about nutrition, and when Sara told her that most of the group from New York were into health and nutrition, Margaret wondered how they would react to her Twinkies!

The Retreat

During our retreat the group asked me to do automatic typing, something I had practiced much earlier in the psychic awareness classes but had discontinued. I had become distrustful of my ability to channel clearly, and my determination not to let my own unconscious impact the typing caused me to let it go. I had seen many people attempt automatic writing and draw information more from their own unconscious mind or their own programming than from a higher source, such as spirit guides. I felt that if I could not be sure of channeling clearly, I did not want to try.

Nevertheless, when this group pressed me I took a leap in the dark and said I would see what came. The women began to ask their questions. I inhaled deeply to let go and focused on becoming receptive to the information so that it could emerge without being blocked by personal thoughts. The group's initial reaction proved so reinforcing that I felt I could continue. In the process of channeling I could feel the gentleness of a female Oriental guide and the flow of a loving energy that I had never before felt.

Later the group did a meditation called the Sacred Pipe Ceremony that Sara's Indian guide had given to her for us. She had recorded it on a cassette tape, and we settled into a circle with a white candle in the center and relaxed into the meditation.

My experience proved to be another harbinger of the return of the tribe, though I did not know it at the time.

I found myself at the edge of a very high cliff and knew that I needed to jump off in faith. I took a deep breath and let myself jump...falling, falling...and then sensed myself being lifted up by guides on either side, one an Oriental female, one a Native American male.

I saw myself being presented to a huge circle at an Indian gathering. I walked around the circle three times in a counterclockwise direction, then three times in a clockwise direction. Then I was taken inside the circle to a chief or a medicine man. This process seemed to be some type of initiation. Words, or a chant, kept running through my mind...Ya-Na-Hene...Ya-Na-Hene...I want to remember these words when I come out of meditation, I thought. Remember these words!

We each took time to share our experience. When I told about the strange words, Dot said, "I wonder if they have any meaning?" I thought not, feeling that the words would prove to be ridiculous if I ever inquired.

But Dot persisted. "Robert and I have given to a charity in South Dakota for many years. It's a Sioux mission. Maybe I can write to them to see if there is a translation." I took solace in the thought that by the time we returned home she would probably have forgotten her proposal.

As we concluded our retreat weekend, Sara gave us a message from her own Indian guide. He said, "You do not yet understand the power of this Circle." Her words produced a movement of energy within me, an emotional reaction that I found startling. I wasn't used to such internal sensations. The Circle? I considered our Circle to be a nice group of women with whom to share inner experiences. Beyond this I could see nothing that merited special consideration.

Three New Members: Deb Nelson, Elaine Goodwin, and Vickie

Following this retreat three other women joined our Circle. The first was Deb Nelsen, whom I met through a client. She was in her thirties and had a freer spirit and stronger assertiveness than the rest of us. Such a strong presence! We enjoyed her unique personality and were aware of how her manner and dress accentuated her independence. Her long, straight black hair fell down her back almost to her waist. A particular connection to Native American teachings was evident in her thinking. She felt especially concerned with the environment. When she spoke to us about it, we could see her anger and frustration. She had practiced recycling before the word "recycle" was in the dictionary and had set up a compost pile and organic garden before they were in style. But in spite of external differences we found our internal connections to be immediate, and Deb quickly fitted into our Circle.

In contrast, Elaine Goodwin, the second of the new members, was a fashionably-dressed petite blond who was politically and socially active in her community. She was a businesswoman, mother, and all-round energetic person whom I had first met in church, where I had been struck by her vivacious personality. Our sons were high school friends and often played basketball together.

We became better acquainted after Elaine interviewed me for an article that she was writing about women-owned businesses. After the traditional interview we moved toward discussing intuitive perception and past lives. Inner promptings pushed me several days later to call Elaine and tell her that my sister-in-law Sara was coming for a visit the following week. I said that Sara did tarot card readings and had some psychic gifts and I wondered if Elaine would like to meet her.

After her visit with Sara, Elaine began meeting weekly with our Circle. At first much of the group discussion remained outside of Elaine's experience but she turned out to be an eager learner and before long her own inner wisdom blossomed. When she spoke she was straightforward, honest, and held our attention.

The third new participant in our Circle was Dot's sister Vickie, whom Dot had encouraged to meet Sara and me. Vickie strikingly resembled her older sister in many ways, including a life-long weight problem and exceptional sensitivity. She seemed much older than her years, perhaps because she had been meditating since she was thirteen. She fit in easily with our Circle and brought a welcome sense of humor.

Dot, Robert, and Anna: Beginning of the Triangle

During the period in which Dot and I had a professional relationship, we had touched on many issues related to her weight and spiritual development and I had worked to help her balance her emotions with her mind and bring these into harmony with her intense sensitivity. After she joined the Circle she was able to move into an increasingly impactful spiritual life, and our relationship changed from that of therapist/client to one of close friends.

Dot's psychic potential was strong and enabled her slowly and cautiously to begin to channel. One day in a trance state she channeled some of the teachings that had been given to her during training in a past life by a medicine woman whom she called Enar. Included in the teachings were instructions about diet that confirmed Sara's earlier channeling of Dot's guides about what foods to eat in this lifetime. Now Enar told Dot that she had an Indian body and should consider this in her choice of foods.

Dot's husband, Robert, was also interested in past lives. This interest was somewhat out of keeping with a highly traditional appearance that reflected his conservative thinking—he usually wore a three-piece suit, and for him informal attire meant casual dress slacks and a collared shirt. He had an average build and receding hairline, and a pair of wire-rimmed glasses sat boldly on his nose.

Robert, in contrast to his generally conservative approach to life, had been practicing meditation for several years, and when he came to me for a regression the process of hypnosis proved easy for him. Instead of return to a past life, however, he first sensed himself in "a learning place," perhaps another name for the interlife where the soul is often exposed to unusual wisdom. There was a fascinating interchange as I asked Robert questions while he was in this state in an effort to learn what would be helpful to his life path.

About this time Robert started taking a massage class and made a new friend of a woman named Anna. Dot was usually quite comfortable with Robert's friends because she felt confident that she could count on his faithfulness to their marriage, but with Anna she found herself disturbed in spite of Robert's openness and apparent honesty. The situation became compounded by Robert's increasing desire to do things separately from Dot and to have friends and activities apart from her.

As time passed, the attraction between Robert and Anna became stronger and Dot felt increasingly threatened. She grew furious when Robert, in an attempt to pacify her, said, "You'd like her. She's a lot like you. She even looks like you." He struggled with his emotions and beliefs. He had never been unfaithful and felt confused by the unexpected feelings stirred up by his friendship with Anna and when he came to me for his first actual regression work his chief thrust was to see if he and Anna had been together before.

> *Robert first found himself as a monk in a garden. A young girl often came to talk with him in the garden and over time fell in love with him. Even though he loved her, he chose to deny love and to stay within the vows he had made. As he passed over into spirit he became aware that he had denied love to one who needed it and also to himself in order to live within rules set by man.*
>
> *Moving into a second lifetime Robert found himself in a Native American life as a medicine man. He saw both Dot and Anna in that life, twin sisters adopted by his father and mother. The three of them apprenticed together with medicine work for the tribe. The one thing that Anna wanted above all else was to have a baby. Robert, who in that life was named Speckled Elk, fathered her child.*

Robert no longer had any doubt as to why he felt so strongly attracted to Anna. He and I talked at length about the situation, and on several occasions he called me as a friend to talk on the phone. Sometimes we lingered over three-hour lunches so that he could talk about his feelings and what was happening.

What we didn't realize was that his material formed one more piece of the puzzle. Many of us had begun to tap into a life in an Indian tribe, but we were not yet aware that it was a shared lifetime. We would begin to realize this connection very shortly.

Chapter IV

Beginning Awareness of the Tribe: 1986 and 1987

The portrait of Silver Eagle, commissioned by my husband as an anniversary gift for me, led to the emergence of our memory of the tribe. Three days after I opened the painting, Sara channeled Silver Eagle's anguish over the massacre, and after that we gradually became aware that the memories of Indian lives that our group recovered referred to the same period and to the same Indian group. One point in Sara's channeling, however, had confused me—the incongruity of a woman becoming chief, and Sara could tell me only that that was what came through. In spite of this ambiguity we became increasingly aware of clues about our shared lifetime as they began to emerge.

Early Clues

The first clues surfaced when I joined DeLaine and Marda for breakfast several days after Sara's channeling. I walked into the nearly-empty restaurant, ordered breakfast, and then told my two friends about the arrival of the painting and about Sara's channeled message. They listened intently.

I handed Sara's message, which I had typed, to DeLaine to read aloud to Marda and was shocked when DeLaine, who consistently kept her emotions under control, began to cry and put her hand over her mouth. Unable to finish reading the paper, she handed it to Marda.

"I think I was his mate," DeLaine sobbed as she tried to compose herself in the restaurant.

What? DeLaine and I had been in a past life together? She had been my mother? I remembered the jokes over the years about the similarity in our looks. *She had been married to this chief in the painting?*

When it is possible I always try to check out the mind's accuracy—I have no wish to be caught by its tricks. So later, not revealing DeLaine's assertion, I wrote to Sara and asked her if she could tell me who Silver Eagle's mate was. Sara wrote back that her friend, Margaret Osborne, was the one referred to as his woman, and DeLaine was the one referred to as his mate.

The weekly meditation circle was at that time meeting at my house. At the next gathering I showed the painting to the others and read the channeled message. I said that even though I did not understand it, I felt that the soul of Silver Eagle needed healing and perhaps we could help in that process during our meditation that night.

At the conclusion of the meditation I opened my eyes and looked at Dot, who sat across from me sobbing. "I blamed him," she said. Then she shared that while in an altered state she had seen that there were five or six of the tribe who chose to go away to a cave to die rather than fight or live under the white man's rule.

Was Dot talking about the Indian lifetime of her recent regression, the one in which she had gone away to a cave to die "rather than eat the white man's poison?" My mind reeled with what had transpired over the past few days. Dot was crying because she had blamed Silver Eagle for the massacre of his people. *Dot was in that lifetime? With DeLaine and me?* Dot's initial regression had occurred weeks before, and now she sobbed because when she went away to the cave she blamed the chief for the impending death of his people.

"Robert knows him, too," Dot said. "I think that Robert needs to have some healing take place between them."

When Robert saw the painting of Silver Eagle some days later, he stared at it for a long time. Then he expressed the need for another regression, and I made only one suggestion as he entered an altered state: he should move to the experience that was most affecting him at this time. He went immediately to an Indian lifetime similar to his previous regression.

> *He spoke of a time of harmony and peace among a tribe of deeply spiritual people who were attuned to the land and Great Spirit. Then discomfort arose as Robert began to see warriors argue about the white man coming. Robert had his own visions but did not trust them. When I asked him if he argued with the chief, he smiled with great gentleness and respect and said, "You don't argue with this chief."*
>
> *With sorrow Robert saw himself and a few others leave the tribe and go away to die rather than fight. He saw the chief say goodby to them and give his blessing. Although by this time Robert had heard the name that we now called the painting, I still asked, "Please tell me the name of the chief."*
>
> *Robert replied softly and with loving emotion, "Silver Eagle."*

My mind began to spin. *Could it be that Robert's Indian incarnation was a lifetime with Dot, me, DeLaine, and Silver Eagle?* Was this possible, I wondered as I sat immobile in the meditation circle trying to piece the puzzle together. By this point, the happenings had gone beyond any logical reasoning. It was beginning to appear that the members of our Circle had been in that incarnation together. We tuned in on more bits and pieces as we meditated together or had individual experiences. Some of us began to learn or remember the Indian names that we had. Sara realized that she had been Silver Eagle's older sister who died at a young age before he became chief. We learned that the tribe was Oglala and lived in what is now the area of the Dakotas.

Dot said that she would like to write the story of the tribe as fiction and asked if she could use the painting for the cover. I agreed, thinking that the history of the tribe would make a fascinating story.

One woman, seeing the painting for the first time, looked at me puzzled as she said, "It looks like Scott." We later learned that Scott was Silver Eagle's father. "The father names the child," I was told. Why would Scott not be the one who immediately knew his name?

We continued in meditation to send love, light, and, from those who needed it, forgiveness, to the soul of Silver Eagle. Many months would pass before we sensed and learned that he had been released from his self-imposed exile.

The Group Regression

Further clues emerged when three months later I offered to do a group regression to see if we could experience that incarnation together. One form of group regression is to allow each individual to experience his own memory, with the therapist asking questions and making suggestions that will fit most lifetimes, but this session would be different. I was going to attempt to take everyone in the circle into the same past life.

As a rule I would not recommend this approach for several reasons. First, I would question how much a person's actual experience is prompted or changed by the comments of others in the room. Also, individual attention is necessary if emotions are to be released and healing take place, and individual monitoring of seven people at once is quite a task for the hypnotherapist. The situation is especially complex when the therapist is a participant in the past-life experience; it becomes more difficult to stay in the therapist role when the therapist hits a powerful emotional memory.

However, our reasons for wishing to attempt a group regression in this particular situation were even more cogent than the drawbacks. Most important was that through individual and separate experiences we already knew of having lived in this life together, and each of us already had a sense of her own experience within the lifetime. Moreover, members of the group had become accustomed to my voice and my direction, as I had already regressed most of them. I knew them all professionally and personally and had been meditating with them for several years. Most compelling was that the fact that the trauma of that lifetime left all of us in need of healing, and there were advantages in seeking this healing together.

In January of 1987 I sat down to prepare myself for the group regression before the women arrived. In an altered state I saw myself as a young girl with my hands tied behind me around a tree. I suddenly remembered my first psychic reading in 1982, in which the psychic described me having a past life as a young Indian where I was used as bait to bring in my father, the chief. He saw the chief ride in, sitting straight and proud. "He looks like a god," the psychic said, and described an Oriental look and a full, long headdress. In the painting the Oriental look of Silver Eagle is quite evident. At the time I received the painting I had forgotten about that reading! But as I sat readying myself for the group, I remembered how the psychic had violently shaken his head to take himself out of the scene, saying, "I don't want to stay there."

That had happened at least five years earlier. I felt shocked suddenly to remember that experience and to realize that the psychic had described a chief who looked like the painting, had referred to him as my father, and had removed himself from the scene of the massacre.

In preparation for the group regression the seven women made themselves comfortable in a circle on the carpeted floor. I began hypnotic induction, indicating that they were to go to what we knew as the lifetime in the tribe of Silver Eagle, if in fact they had been there. Instead of any other suggestions, I played a tape of Indian chants and allowed each of them to continue to relax and begin to have her own experience as I monitored the room.

Using either her present name or her Indian identity, I addressed whichever woman appeared to be perceiving most strongly at any given moment.

Janet: *Marda, describe to me what you are seeing, sensing, or feeling.*

Marda: *I see the men dancing around, and you and I sitting as little girls on the ground with our legs crossed, watching, and I just got a feeling that I loved you like a sister.*

Janet: *Okay. The men are dancing…is there anything else that you see in this scene that you want to mention?*

Marda: *Just the tepees, and the fire…dancing around the fire.*

Janet: Good. Is there anyone who is in this place and whom you can describe more fully in this particular scene—the men dancing, the fire...?

Elaine: I see the men dancing. I feel like I'm on someone's back, wrapped up. But it seems like I'm on a man's back, which doesn't seem right...but he's moving, he's not dancing, but he's...his body, I can feel it moving to the music.

Janet: Do you want to describe that scene any more?

Elaine: Just that I can feel his body moving under mine, I'm on his back and I can see what I'm wrapped up in. It's plain and soft, it's like a hide, but decorated. It has different colors and there are beads across the...like leather thongs with beads on them. And I've got little paunchy cheeks, and the men are dancing. I can see that—I can feel it more than anything.

Janet: Okay. Is there anyone else who can be in this scene and elaborate more on what they are sensing or feeling?

DeLaine: Silver Eagle is not dancing—he's watching, very proud.

Janet: Is there anyone around Silver Eagle?

DeLaine: The fire is a very bright light.

Janet: Dot, what are you seeing?

Dot: The baby is on my back—and I wish I were a man.

Janet: Okay.

Dot: I'm preparing food and listening and moving with the music as much as I can, as much as I am permitted.

Janet: You are not permitted to dance?

Dot: I am to make the food. This is the men's celebration.

Janet: Why do you wish that you were a man?

Dot: Men do the important things, in my view.

Janet: Name those important things to me.

Dot: The hunt. They guide the spiritual way for the tribe. They protect the tribe.

Janet: Is this your baby on your back?

Dot: No.

Janet: Whose baby is on your back?

Dot: This is the child of my brother and my sister...my foster brother.

Janet: What is this celebration for? Anyone. Why this celebration? What is going on?

Deb: *I think it was a good hunt. I see myself with a spear, just going with the music…my leg was shaking before.*

Janet: *And you are dancing with the music?*

Deb: *I wasn't dancing around as much as in place.*

Janet: *Okay, with the spear in your hand?*

Deb: *Yes.*

Janet: *Can you describe yourself more to us?*

Deb: *I can't see my face. I can see buckskin. I see fringe…a piece of buffalo fur, like a tail on the end of the spear.*

Janet: *So it was a good hunt. Is Windflower there?*

Vickie: *(Shakes her head no.)*

Janet: *You do not sense yourself being there. Okay.*

Vickie: *I just sense the emotions of happiness of the good hunt.*

Deb: *I keep taking glimpses of the baby; I can see the fat face. I'm peeking and teasing it.*

DeLaine: *I'm getting an impression of women standing in the background by the tepees.*

Janet: *What are the women doing?*

DeLaine: *We're very busy preparing food and observing while we're preparing…the joy of the dancing, yet busy, moving constantly.*

Janet: *What kind of food is being prepared? Anyone.*

Elaine: *I smell meat roasting—I thought it was deer.*

Deb: *I see buffalo.*

Elaine: *I feel the warmth of the dancer's body and the warmth of the fire. I smell…I'm hungry all the time…and I smell the meat roasting. The women are talking about the food… something yellow.*

Deb: *It's corn.*

Janet: *Is the baby aware of Flaming Arrow's attention to her?*

Elaine: *(Nodding yes.) I can see other people too, kind of watching what's going on with us. He has his hand near my nose or my face.*

Janet: *Joyce, as Red Hawk, do you have any sense of being there right now?*

Joyce: *(Shakes her head no.)*

Janet: *Okay. I'm going to turn on the music, and I want you to stay in this lifetime and move forward in time to a particular event or experience that is in some way important to you. It may be the same as others see, or it may be a scene quite different. Stay with your own vision; stay with your own thoughts, even as you hear another speaking.*

Starting the music, I counted slowly as time passed, and then I turned off the Indian chants.

Janet: *Elaine, what are you experiencing now?*

Elaine: *I'm on the ground, I'm not as wrapped up as I was before.*

Janet: *What are you doing lying on the ground?*

Elaine: *I feel the rocks…I'm not sure what's going on, but I don't feel good…people are near me. I see red, red around me.*

Janet: *Okay, I want you to stay with that for a while. Marda, what are you sensing or feeling?*

Marda: *I'm hearing horses somewhere…we're together, that's all I get.*

Janet: *Okay, do you have sense of how old you are?*

Marda: *Ten, twelve maybe.*

Janet: *Are we alone or is anyone with us?*

Marda: *We're alone.*

Janet: *And how do you feel?*

Marda: *Happy. I just keep getting a sense of the closeness we had.*

Janet: *Good. Joyce, do you have any impressions?*

Joyce: *(Shaking her head no.) But I did see a gorgeous face, and he was shining in the firelight, and his skin was a beautiful bronze color, and he looked like a postcard…a headdress.*

Janet: *Okay, Windflower, do you have any impressions that are in your mind?*

Vickie: *(Shakes her head no.)*

Elaine: *There's a circle of rocks, big rocks in a circle…a beautiful circle of rocks, and I'm leaning against one of those rocks.*

Janet: *Are the people near you?*

Elaine: *Yes, they're tired.*

Janet: *What have they been doing?*

Elaine: *I don't know. They seem confused over…one is lying next to me or sitting next to me. They've been here before—this is a place to go.*

Janet: *Flaming Arrow, what impressions do you have?*

Deb: *I think we're asking for guidance. I think the Council is there. And I see the rocks too; it's a Medicine Wheel, definitely. And Silver Eagle is passing the pipe, asking for guidance on whether the people should move or not.*

Janet: *Why are they considering a move?*

Deb: *The invasion by white men. There's an argument going on between some of them, saying, "Why should we have to move? We take care of the land, the land takes care of us. This is no one's land, no one's to own. Where are we going to hunt?"*

Janet: *And so Silver Eagle is passing the pipe to ask for Divine Guidance, to ask for guidance from Great Spirit.*

Deb: *There is a lot of tension.*

Janet: *And how does Flaming Arrow feel at this point?*

Deb: *Arguing, but not arguing with Silver Eagle.*

Elaine: *Some people are saying that if we leave them alone they'll leave us alone...there is room for all of us. I keep seeing that red.*

Janet: *Is the entire tribe here, or a portion of the tribe?*

Elaine: *They're not all here.*

Deb: *No, I don't think so, either...there might be four or five and then the Council.*

Janet: *Does anyone have an impression of what that red is?*

Elaine: *It's on the other side of me, like a part of the pipe, but it isn't the pipe. (We later determined that the pipe had red feathers attached to it.)*

Janet: *Dot, what are your impressions?*

Dot: *Standing Tree is locked in her visions. She sits, is just... almost like in a coma, locked in her visions of what is to come, cannot escape.*

Janet: *Is she with this group of people, or is she away? Where is she?*

Dot: *With the group...but not participating.*

Janet: *Okay, I understand.*

Deb: *I hear words, "We have to eat. We cannot let them drive us away from our hunting ground."*

Janet: *Is White Fawn here or in another place?*

DeLaine: *White Fawn is back, preparing food, constantly preparing food, working constantly.*

Janet: *Before we leave this place, as each of you is in your own scene, is there any other impression that anyone has within*

	her own scene that she wants to mention before we move on?
Elaine:	*There's one man who's always mean to me. He holds a fire in front of me.*
Janet:	*Do you have any more information about this man?*
Elaine:	*He's a big man, long dark hair. He's very handsome.*
Janet:	*Why do you suppose he does that?*
Elaine:	*I don't know; but I like him.*
Janet:	*Why do you like him?*
Elaine:	*Everyone likes him....*
Janet:	*Any other impressions from anyone in whatever scene you happen to be in?*
DeLaine:	*I'm taking care of the children...all the children.*
Deb:	*I see myself walking away, leaning against a rock, walking out of the Council, saying that we must stay and stand and take care of ourselves, where we know best.*
Marda:	*I sense the tension. I think we were riding together to feel some freedom from the heaviness.*
Janet:	*Okay.*
Vickie:	*My chest hurts a lot.*
Janet:	*Why is that, do you know?*
Vickie:	*(Shakes her head no.)*
Janet:	*Okay. Now we're going to move forward in time. Just relax, relax. Moving forward in time within this same lifetime...to a particular event, situation or experience that is in some way important to bring forward to the consciousness at this time. Allow your minds to relax, and as I count from one to three you will move forward in time to an event that is important to be brought forward now, to the consciousness of this circle. Number one, number two, number three. You are there now. Allow the impressions to come. And I'll ask anyone who is getting strong impressions to speak first.*

The entire vibration in the room changed.

Dot:	*I can no longer speak.*
Janet:	*Why can Standing Tree no longer speak?*
Dot:	*I will not speak. I have lost my sister. They have sent her away.*
Janet:	*What has happened to your sister?*

Dot:	*White soldiers got her.*
Janet:	*Were you there?*
Dot:	*No, but I saw. I see too much.*
Janet:	*I'm going to go to the baby. What is the baby sensing?*
Elaine:	*(Her lower lip moves out in a child-like manner and she starts to cry.)*
Janet:	*It's okay...just let the impressions come....*
Elaine:	*(Sobbing.) I'm...in...a hole....*
Janet:	*You're in a hole in the ground?*
Elaine:	*(Nods yes.)*
Janet:	*Are you alone?*
Elaine:	*(Shakes her head no.) ...but...she's dying...(referring to her mother, Anna, and sobbing)...she's trying to comfort...but she's too...she can't do anything. They won't hurt me. I don't want her to go away; there's no one else.*
Janet:	*Now, I'm going to have Elaine leave this scene if she so chooses...and I want the others to stay with the impressions you have. (Repeating instructions.)*
Elaine:	*(Whispering.) ...they're walking around with the horses. She's gone now...gone, she was too weak to stay here. They're moving around up there. They're talking about what to do....*
Janet:	*(Repeating instructions to Elaine.) ...and I'm going to go to Dot. Tell me the impressions that you are receiving.*
Dot:	*She should have been a man.*
Janet:	*How would men have acted differently?*
Dot:	*This would not have happened to her.*
Janet:	*In what way do you mean this?*
Dot:	*We are weak.*
Janet:	*Weak in what way?*
Dot:	*Physically weak.*
Janet:	*And does this make a difference?*
Dot:	*(Nodding yes.) To fight, to hit back. Not just see dreams, but act. I don't know what is a dream and what is real. I haven't for a long time.*
Janet:	*I'm going to ask Red Hawk. Does Red Hawk have any impressions?*
Joyce:	*(Shakes her head no.)*
Janet:	*Does Flaming Arrow have any impressions?*
Deb:	*Just insisting that our people are dying by our restraint.*

Janet: *And to whom are you speaking?*

Deb: *Silver Eagle. We need to make a decision. I not only see our people being starved, I see our people sick from what I think is smallpox. I see a face, a pitted face of scared... there is a woman who had two children by me, and the woman is sick. Small children.*

Janet: *What is the feeling of Flaming Arrow at this point?*

Deb: *A sense of falling apart. We have lost many warriors. We need to move, we need to be somewhere safe.*

Janet: *How have we lost the warriors?*

Deb: *Fighting, ambush. I feel a sense of urgency. We need to move now. We are not a strong tribe anymore. We will be snuffed out. A sense of survival—take what we have and go...move out...(raising her voice) and leave us alone!*

Janet: *What is Little Feather sensing?*

Marda: *We're helping the women packing...(voice shaking). We're confused, we don't understand what's going on. We were always together.*

Janet: *What kinds of things are we packing?*

Marda: *Bits of food, clothing...it's not very clear.*

Janet: *Okay. Does Windflower have any impressions?*

Vickie: *I'm uncomfortable.*

Janet: *Why are you uncomfortable?*

Vickie: *Pain in my chest, like a weight.*

Janet: *What is the weight in your chest?*

Vickie: *I don't see anything.*

Janet: *Okay, allow yourself to be more at ease and more comfortable. What do you see, Dot?*

Dot: *I see the end.*

Janet: *Before I ask you to move into that scene, I'm going to ask White Fawn...where are you and what impressions do you have?*

DeLaine: *There are men coming on horses. People are running.*

Janet: *Are they white men or Indians?*

DeLaine: *(More fear in her voice.) They're the white soldiers. The tepees are falling over...we need to run. They're knocking us down. (Puts her hand to her neck.) My neck!*

Janet: *Your neck is bothering you?*

DeLaine: *Yes... (Her conscious mind makes a connection.) I've never liked anything tight around my neck.*

Janet:	Dot, what is happening to you?
Dot:	I'm not there—I see it.
Janet:	Tell me what you see.
Dot:	I see (tears streaming down her face) what is happening to the bodies of my loved ones. I see hate...and it overtakes me. We have not known this...it's poison. I do not understand how other humans can destroy...this way...there is no heart...it is...better to die...than to live this way...we cannot live like this...they do not understand the role of Great Spirit.
Janet:	Windflower, what are you feeling?
Vickie:	...hard to breathe...

I gave instructions to Vickie to relax and allow her breathing to return to normal. After making certain that Vickie's breathing had stabilized, my attention moved to the others in the room.

Janet:	Little Feather, what is happening?
Marda:	I'm scared. (Voice trembling.) We're holding tight to each other. We're just real scared.
Janet:	Okay. Are there any more impressions from White Fawn?
DeLaine:	I'm worried about the children...get the children...what will happen to the children...I won't be there to take care of them.
Janet:	Can either White Fawn or Standing Tree tell me where Silver Eagle is at this point?
Dot:	He's in the middle...he's still fighting...as if...protected by special armor.... He and another warrior back to back.

At this point I saw the scene vividly of my father in the middle, fighting. I thrust my hand over my mouth to keep my own emotions inside. I did some fast internal talk. *Stay in control, Janet, you're the hypnotherapist who is leading this regression; seven others are in a hypnotic state—you can't lose it now!* Within a split second I spoke in a normal voice.

Janet:	Before we leave this scene and this lifetime, I want to say that if there is additional insight that is important to be brought from the unconscious to the conscious mind, it will

> *come in the hours or days ahead in a way that is*
> *comfortable to you. While in this place, are there any last*
> *impressions being sensed that should be brought forward,*
> *anyone?*

DeLaine: *(With much sadness and pain in her voice.) Why...did they*
> *do this?*

As I began to bring the women slowly back into the room, I sensed Silver Eagle's presence and asked Dot if she could receive and channel his message.

Chief: *You have accomplished here very important purpose. While*
> *painful to re-live, you have cleansed the soul of memories*
> *held tightly, but best let go, as I have had to do. Some of*
> *the memory, the memory of the love, the sharing, the joyful*
> *times, can now be re-lived. Nourish that. Discard the*
> *bitterness, the hurt, and move on. We now can move*
> *together. I feel welcome in your Circle. And you are wel-*
> *come, again...(tears streaming down her face)...in my*
> *heart. I am very proud of my people.*

Deb: *That is why you are Chief. Your heart is big enough to*
> *have many many gatherings and dances and many people.*

Chief: *We will dance again. We will celebrate as we have*
> *celebrated before. We will renew Mother Earth. My*
> *daughter, this is a very good thing. And my mate, I extend*
> *my heart to you. We can speak again now. My heart is very*
> *happy.*

I continued to give instructions to the women to return fully into the room and the present time, feeling the healing that had taken place, "as if a great weight has been lifted from our shoulders, from our hearts, and from our minds."

In discussion afterward, we realized that Vickie's lessened ability to perceive was due to her being old and senile at that time. Also, the heaviness and difficulty in breathing resulted, she sensed, from a horse falling on her during the battle; that is how she died.

Joyce had been an old man named Red Hawk during the time period that we explored. Red Hawk was not at the Medicine Wheel and he was one who went to the cave to die. So, Joyce's unconscious memories did not include the massacre.

Elaine was the only one who survived. As an infant she was found by a white soldier and taken home to his wife. But this child felt so sad and out of place that she refused food and died.

Chapter V

Trauma in Our Circle: 1987-1988

I had been told that before the end of my present life the people of our small tribe who are now incarnate would come to me. This process now appeared to be taking place and our healing had begun. Our Circle had met weekly at my house during the years from 1985 to 1988. Together and individually, our spiritual paths had taken many turns. In the group regression we had done what we could to release stored emotion, and now we moved on to more immediate concerns.

Transitions

Marda and her husband had separated and she was devastated. After over twenty-five years of marriage she was now trying to live alone. At first she could only cry. Eventually she chose to go back to school, feeling that she needed a career to support herself. She made top grades, and with a sheer determination and fight that she never realized she had inside her "passive personality," Marda moved out into the work force.

Deb had been divorced for several years and was now in the midst of a difficult karmic love relationship. In addition, she found her nursing career incredibly frustrating. Her anger rose as she struggled to mesh her beliefs in holistic health and self-responsibility in one's healing with the structured medical establishment.

Our meditation times often began and ended with plenty of personal sharing. We joked that the reason Marda had named our meditation group the "Circle of Love" was not necessarily because we were so loving—as we had first thought—but instead that Love was what we were learning. Vickie, we agreed, would learn some of the lessons through our experiences...and at her young age could have her act together *before* marriage.

DeLaine was experiencing her own trauma. From the energetic "wonder woman" who never became ill, she fell sick with colds and congestion, coughing and wheezing that she could not shake. Going to doctors and taking antibiotics did not help. She had trouble breathing, a problem that lasted for two years. Whenever she stayed away from the barn and milking, the congestion eased a little. It was as though her body were speaking to her. For the person who always "did it all," it became very difficult for her to admit to herself that she had to stay out of the barn and give up working on the farm. Eventually she determined that she needed to find alternative healing methods for her problems and began that process.

Some years earlier I had come across the book *Body-Mind* by Dr. Ken Dychtwald and when I saw the diagram related to foot reflexology I said out loud, "DeLaine has to have this book." From that time on DeLaine studied reflexology, polarity balancing, and other forms of body-healing. These practices seemed to trigger a wisdom already inside her. When she could no longer work on the farm she began to take clients in her home for bodywork.

Joyce, the astrologer, had her own issues with which she had coped for years, issues related to the alcoholism of her family members. She continued to give us information about the energy of the planets and how each of us was being affected. For instance, she told DeLaine that she was in competition with her husband. Marda learned from Joyce, to her dismay, that her marital problems would not improve for two years, a prediction that proved to be correct.

Repetition of the Triangle in the Indian Lifetime

Dot had resisted hearing that Robert and Anna had a compulsive attraction, but this, also, was proving to be correct, and as time went on, the attraction between Robert and Anna became stronger. As Dot and Robert struggled with their marriage and what this new situation meant, I met with them both individually and together. Though they had no children, after a twenty-three year marriage they were attached to each other and neither of them had expected anything like this would ever happen.

Dot called me almost daily as she tried to cope with what was going on between Robert and her. She assumed that if Robert had fallen in love with Anna, he could not still love her. I tried to help her understand that she was operating out of a limited concept of love; it is possible to love more than one person. I knew that Dot was capable of expanding her mind beyond the programming and conditioning of her society. Otherwise I would not have spoken to her in the manner I did. "You cannot control whom he loves, Dot," I said. "You have nothing to say about that. Putting limitations on whom another person can love comes out of possessiveness. One soul cannot limit the freedom of another, especially in love."

Eventually, when Robert was about to leave on an extended business trip, Dot told him that he needed to explore what he wanted. She could not stay in the house alone and went to a friend's empty house to stay for three months. Unable to separate out her energies, thoughts, or "self," Dot wrote to Robert daily while he was away and meditated twice a day, sending him energy. At the same time she struggled to discover who she was and what she liked to do by herself. She drove to my house for weekly meditation. The comfort of her friends in the Circle and her psychic opening and spiritual path kept her world from falling apart completely.

Dot had encouraged Robert to go to a psychologist to help "break his addiction," but she came to recognize that this was not effective; Robert and Anna were back together. In time, Dot and Robert sold their house and began to live apart. Again and again Dot said to me, "If he goes with Anna, he won't do what he came here to do." She remembered a belief that she had held in the tribe, that the "medicine power among the three was broken" when Robert and Anna had the baby. Dot recovered more memories of that earlier life and of her twin sister, whom she now recognized to be Anna. "His spiritual path will be affected," she said to me in alarm. More years would pass before we fully understood that whatever one is doing, each individual is on his own spiritual path.

Life Lessons

Elaine was going through growth spurts in business and psychic sensitivity. Using the power of her mind and intuition, she served as a role model for everyone around her—people wondered how she could do it all. At the same time, she was going through some difficulties with one of her children, as well as with the children from her third marriage.

And me? One evening before meditation started, Marda said, "Janet, everyone else is going through all of these life lessons. When are you going to have your turn?" Marda's comment surprised me. She knew what my personal situation had been. Years before, my elderly mother and father had moved into our large 17-room Victorian house and lived with us. During the last two years of his life my father had Alzheimer's disease; he did not know us or where he was. After his death my mother had several more strokes and died two years later. *When would I have my turn at life's lessons?* As I apparently had always done, I continued to reveal only the "perfect" image; I was still giving others the impression that I handled everything with no problems.

Members of our group contributed to one another's healing every step of the way. The years of love and support, of listening and caring, of time given, cannot be measured. As one grew, we all grew. As one experienced what we came to call a life "lesson" and moved through it with a new view and expanded her spirituality, we all learned. Connecting to our spiritual selves made a significant difference. We gave one another "help," not sympathy. There was no blaming, whether of the Circle member, the husband, the boss, or the other person involved. We challenged one another to grow in love and in spiritual awareness. We grew by leaps and bounds, and our lessons came even faster.

Through the summers of 1987 and 1988 my business sponsored retreat weekends with a team of holistic health professionals. The small-group intensives proved to be exciting and rewarding both to the attendees and to the staff. Although neither DeLaine nor Dot worked on the permanent staff, occasionally they would come out to assist.

Marilyn

Our last retreat weekend was in September. DeLaine and Dot were there, and Sara came for a long-overdue visit. We met Marilyn Terwilliger, a woman in her late 30's who later said she had reached the point of determining whether she chose to live or die (she had attempted suicide previously). As I looked at Marilyn, I saw a combination of hardness from life and child-like innocence. Her long, wavy strawberry blond hair falling down her back reflected the free image she portrayed.

"The reason that I came to the retreat was to meet you, Janet," she said. "I was looking for a hypnotherapist, and when I saw you I knew it would be okay." Marilyn had been in traditional therapy for several years. She had strong psychic ability clouded by painful childhood memories and stored emotion, but she was aware of some of the memories that she needed to re-live. At one of our first sessions she began to enter an altered state and opened her eyes to ask me, "Are you afraid?" I smiled at her and answered with an honest authority, "I can handle it."

For the first few weeks Marilyn hovered in a precarious state, and Dot went to help her. I felt thankful that Dot was available, and I knew that Marilyn could not be in better hands to continue healing and growth in the spiritual dimension. Marilyn said, "I have worked for years to heal my body. Then I worked to heal my mind. Now I need help to heal my spirit."

At the end of the first week of helping Marilyn, Dot said to me, "I've met Enar." This remark surprised me. *Enar? The medicine*

woman in the Indian life? Was Dot saying that Marilyn was Enar? As
I usually do, I "filed it" in my memory bank and took a wait-and-see
attitude.

Even though I had closed my business for a year and was "in
hiding" by this time, I took Marilyn as my only client. Her steps in
healing over the next year and a half challenged me, as Dot and a few
others had done, to go beyond the limitations of my training and to
trust myself and the guidance that I received.

Several psychics had perceived over the years that I had a master
guide, first in the background and now strongly connected with my
energy. They called him "The Mind Master."

> *The Mind Master is the master of the mind—not mastered
> by the mind. You go beyond.*

Many times I had trouble moving beyond my mind's
programming, but often I simply had no choice. Nothing in my
training had prepared me for what had begun to happen in my life
and work. No question about it, I *had* to move beyond my own mind
in order to help the people who were coming to me now. I soon
learned that I had to get "myself" out of the way, and the guidance
was there.

I continued to work with Marilyn and Dot, and, as with the
Circle, we took turns helping to heal one another. As I watched
Marilyn help with Dot's healing, I agreed that Dot's initial impression
had been correct—Marilyn was a medicine woman—Marilyn was
Enar.

Chapter VI

The Cabin—A Vision Quest:
August 1988-August 1989

It became time for "Miss Perfect" to be seen as less than perfect. In August 1988 Scott and I sold our large house and chose to live apart for a year. While I was packing and emptying everything in our house to move, I came across the tiny silver headdress—the charm that had been given to me by an employee. I had thought that I had thrown it away. Now, as I held it in my hand, I felt dumbfounded at the symbol that it held for me—given to me *seven years previously.*

For this new period in my life I closed my business, moved to a different town, and lived in a cabin in the woods—to be alone. I ordered an unlisted phone number and told only my family and friends in the Circle where I lived. I asked all of them not to drop in. For many years our home had been like a revolving door of people and community activities and action and business, and after a lifetime of pleasing everyone and smiling, I needed time with me. Now as I look back, I think of this time as my "Vision Quest," although I didn't realize it at the time.

I began to have a strong feeling that it was time to change the name of my business and create a new logo. I struggled with this choice for a long time; the name came one day in meditation with the Circle. Breakthroughs to the Unconscious® would be the new name—and I knew that first I would have to make deeper breakthroughs into my own unconscious mind before I could take the next step in helping others to heal. I saw my hands reaching up, breaking the ropes that bound them. My logo was later designed using my own hands. It related to three past incarnations where my hands had been bound—including the one as a young girl in the Oglala tribe.

"The blockages in your unconscious mind
prevent you from being free—as
surely as if your hands were tied with ropes."
— *Janet Cunningham*

For my retreat I chose an external environment that reflected my internal circumstances, a place of seclusion to work on myself and delve deeply into my own unconscious. Large flagstone steps led down a path to a small cabin surrounded by trees and natural growth of brush and wildflowers. Pine walls throughout made the inside quite dark. Two sliding glass doors in the living room brought in light and allowed me to enjoy nature's beauty outside. For our year of living apart I had taken the small amount of rustic furniture and Scott had taken the Victorian furniture.

During my first two months "in hiding," our Circle met at Elaine's house. Robert joined us, driving to the Penn-York Valley from Corning, and Vickie continued to drive in from Ithaca. But gradually it seemed that all of us were going through situations that called for individual and separate energy. So, although we kept in touch and occasionally one or two of us would have breakfast or lunch, we no longer met as a Circle to meditate together.

Occasionally I visited DeLaine for massage and reflexology. Her abilities and psychic sensitivity had begun to expand. As she worked on my body she told me that there was very little energy in my hands. This perception corresponded with what a friend had seen—an aura of light-energy around my entire body except my hands.

Dot and DeLaine in our work together often voiced frustration with my lack of emotional expression. They said that I had shut down my feelings and emotions. I knew that I hadn't shut down my feelings—but as for expressing my emotions, they were right. DeLaine's comments on the lack of emotional energy in my body made me sound like a robot. Somehow I knew that I had locked many of my emotions in my mental self, and breaking through them was one of my "tasks" during this time alone.

The year alone brought healing to my emotional self. Without the outside distractions that had always been part of my life, my time alone at the cabin was a pleasant contrast of enjoyment, self-discovery, and incredible inner turmoil. Understanding the need to accept my emotional being, I found myself gradually "feeling" my emotions. In the past I had automatically stuffed them down, ignored them or used logic to move away from emotion. This internal fight with my own personality could only be done alone.

At the end of the year of my retreat, I moved back with Scott. I located a small office space in a professional building and began taking clients again on a part-time basis while continuing my own inner work and my research in levels of consciousness and obesity.

I thought I had been ready to "come out of hiding" when I began taking clients again. However if my external movement (new office space) again reflected my Inner Self, I was "going deeper"—into a basement. The professional building was attractively positioned on Route 17C on the Susquehanna River. Entering by the side door, a client walked downstairs to a space for aerobics classes with one full-mirrored wall and a lovely kitchenette. A licensed massage practitioner and I rented office space for appointments. My tiny room was large enough for the hypnosis chair, a maple sitting-chair for me, and stereo equipment. It had no windows. A few credentials and pictures completed the décor for undistracted sessions.

Since I now lived with Scott in Elmira and drove to Owego, New York, I decided to work only part time and devote my primary energy to our relationship.

The following fall I kept getting mental messages that I should now put the Indian headdress charm on a silver bracelet that Dot had given me. I smiled at the thought of my ego getting carried away with the message of *"Now you take your place as Chief."* Nevertheless, I put it on and was guided to *call the tribe together.* Our Circle had not met regularly for at least a year. The message kept coming until I could no longer ignore it.

I phoned Dot. She said, "I've been feeling like we were to get together—the Chief calls the gathering." I told Dot that I felt there was to be some type of meditation ritual, but I had no idea why we were to get together. Dot later said that she had seen pictures of a healing ritual in which she would use the hand-made drum that Robert had given her.

Each woman felt happy at the idea of getting together; it had been a long time. We met at Marilyn's house, each bringing a dish to share for dinner. Before we ate we sat in a circle in the living room. I told them about the charm, explaining that I did not fully understand why we were to get together but that there was to be a meditation led by the two women in the tribe who had been medicine women at that time. I repeated to the Circle what I had said on many occasions, "Today there is no chief and no medicine woman. Now, we are all chiefs and we are all medicine women."

Marilyn had asked us to bring partially-burned candles as a symbol of bringing wood for the fire. As she gathered the candles, she assembled them on a metal plate in the center of the room and lit each one. We commented on the unusual colors. Instead of white, orchid, or pink that we usually used, we had brought candles of green, orange, brown—fall colors. Vickie pointed out that the date I had nonchalantly selected was the fall equinox, according to Joyce an excellent time for a gathering. It was just one more of the "coincidences" that continued to surprise us.

We closed our eyes for a group meditation, and after a while Dot began to drum and Marilyn used the rattles that had been given to her as a gift. Nothing had been planned—it was all spontaneous. These sounds seemed to carry us back to a time long ago—a time of beauty and simplicity.

Eventually the sounds stopped. Some of the women kept their eyes closed to stay in the space. I chose to open my eyes (my curiosity wouldn't let me do otherwise) and I watched Marilyn take over the ceremony. Wrapped in a white elk skin, she began moving around the circle to one woman at a time, connecting with them. Marilyn had again become the medicine woman. I watched her actions with each one. Tears ran down her face as she touched one's feet, another's hands, cleaned another's aura. By the time she came to me, Marilyn was sobbing. She tore off a piece from her elk skin and placed it in my hand. As she moved on to Elaine, she removed the skin from herself and wrapped it around Elaine, as if wrapping a baby in a soft, safe place. To Dot, Marilyn gave a symbol of handing over her power—something that had not been done in that lifetime.

Afterward we talked. Marilyn had been in an altered state and was not always fully aware of what she had been doing, although she had felt the sorrow and pain in each one as she went around the Circle. "When I got to Janet," she said, "I thought I would go hysterical."

So the time of separation and retreat came full circle and moved our group back to a deepened perception of a time of mutual suffering.

Chapter VII

New Friends: December 1989 to July 1990

A pleasant development in our understanding of the tribe occurred shortly after this. A male voice explained that he had been born in Italy and made an appointment, spelling his name for me: Orazio Salati. He said that a friend, who was a nun and former client of mine, recommended that he see me for a regression back to his childhood.

"Roz" was an attractive man in his early forties, five feet eight with a medium build and an auburn beard and moustache and receding hairline. He had a friendly and likeable manner and a bright smile. I learned that he was an artist and a teacher at an area high school. When he came on December 21, 1989, he brought two people with him and asked if they could accompany him into the room. I agreed, inviting them for an introduction and explanation of the process of hypnosis and childhood regression. I explained that they could step out when we did the regression, but I was aware that they were close friends and Roz wanted their support.

One of these friends was Kate Paul, a nun who worked as Director of Religious Education. As a friend she knew of the personal situation that had prompted Roz's call. She was a tall woman in her mid-forties with fair skin and silver-grey hair that she wore in a stylish short upsweep on the sides. She had a pleasant and quiet but direct way about her.

As I shook hands with the third person, I was struck with the dissimilarity of this young man in the friendship threesome.

Twenty-nine years old and looking much younger, Michael Ranucci had dark hair and skin, matched only by his dark brown eyes. He was five feet eleven with a slim build.

As Roz talked I could see that he maintained no barriers to an openness with his friends. Thus when we began the regression I did not feel the need to ask them to step out and they sat quietly as Roz moved back into his childhood memories. I was aware throughout our session that Michael felt Roz's emotions more than Roz did, and at the conclusion, Kate's nodding head reinforced my suggestions. We talked afterward, and Roz welcomed input from his friends.

Michael took me off guard when he asked, "How much do you use your psychic ability when you do hypnosis?" I admit to working with psychic people, not to having any particular abilities myself. I looked across the room at this young man and smiled. Somehow I knew I couldn't fool him; he could get right at the heart of a matter...real fast. I found myself being very open with these three new people in my office, and when I hesitated in referring to past lives Kate urged me on, letting me know that I did not need to hold back with them.

I looked at Roz in the hypnosis chair, and I saw a powerful creativity that he had not even begun to tap. In spite of all his artistic endeavors to date—and there were many—I saw so much more! And, I saw fear. As with other clients, I didn't know if he would be able to move through the fear, to free himself and release his creativity. He made an appointment for further work after the holidays. We gave each other a hug, pleased with his initial progress and happily looking forward to our next session.

As we said goodbye, I walked past Michael and asked spontaneously, "So, how much have you developed *your* psychic ability?" I got a surprised and rather non-committal reply.

Although I knew that Kate would not accompany Roz at his next visit, I hoped that we would meet again. She seemed happy with what had transpired and gave me a hug of appreciation.

The next day Michael would be flying back to Florida where he lived. I had no reason to expect ever to come in contact with him. But as we hugged, I looked at him and said, "I'll see you again."

Roz

Roz returned regularly and we worked together on a variety of issues, one of which was the cause of headaches that he had suffered for over sixteen years. He had undergone every test medical science offered, only to be told that there was "nothing wrong." Sessions with psychologists and psychiatrists provided no more answers. Since he had eliminated possible physical problems, I sensed that his problems could relate to the area of "vision and psychic seeing." Even though he already used his artistic talents, his abilities extended far beyond his current work. I sensed that he had been blocking his "third eye"[1] for years.

In an attempt to find the cause of his problems we did a past-life regression. He first recalled a lifetime as a male lawyer in colonial times, either in the United States or France. Afterward he wondered if he could have made it all up.

He did not wonder or make that statement after his second regression, when Roz saw himself as female, a Native American:

> She was standing on a very high rock, reaching upward and holding her newborn high as she thanked Great Spirit. "My arms are holding the baby upward to the sky." She introduced the newborn to the four directions, as well as to the trees, animals, and rocks. But as we moved ahead in time, she returned to the village and saw destruction. Her warrior husband had been killed.
>
> In the next experience she was on her knees, frantically digging through a grave site with her hands. "We do not do this. Our people are not put into the ground—our spirits must be free."
>
> She and her son were taken in by another tribe, where she lived out the last of her years. As we moved to the end of that life I heard a loving description of the child, now about 13 years old. "His name is Running Deer...his father lives through him; he looks just like his father."
>
> I asked if she could tell me what her name was, and Roz replied, hesitating, "Angel..." and then his conscious mind

became alert as he said, "That doesn't sound like an Indian name."

"If it's important, it will come," I replied, not wanting his conscious mind to interfere with the trance state.

At the end of that life she was old and ready to leave to be with her mate.

Roz made several deep connections through this regression. He spoke of having a long interest in Native American culture. His art depicted that interest in many ways—through Indian jewelry, Native American pottery, and tapestry. His first tapestry was from a Navajo design.

Roz recognized his son of that life to be Michael, and even though he had hesitated on his own name, he had no doubt that Michael's name was Running Deer.

Many of my clients have retrieved Indian lifetimes, usually with no thought on my part that they were connected to the Silver Eagle tribe. But with Roz it was different. I felt that he had been a member of that tribe. His regression, however, did not fit with what I knew to be true—there had been no survivors, other than the baby, and this baby chose to leave her body when white people took her. In Roz's regression he witnessed the destruction and then was taken in by another tribe.

I felt that though this was certainly possible in the Silver Eagle incarnation, I didn't feel sure. I was looking at the facts as they had been expressed through regressions. I chose not to mention the tribe to Roz because it wasn't important. His regression had given him the information that was valuable for him; it was successful.

Kate

Roz's friend Kate had come to me a few times for counseling after having decided to leave her religious community. I felt that Kate would find DeLaine's bodywork beneficial, and I gave her DeLaine's business card. After their first session together, DeLaine called me excitedly. "Janet," she said, "I think Kate was a member of the tribe."

I could certainly believe that any of these three people were, as I had felt an instant closeness with them from the moment I had met them. Once again, however, I took a wait-and-see attitude.

We had several counseling appointments before Kate felt ready to try a past-life regression. Then I directed her unconscious mind to move to an event or experience that was affecting her. With no other suggestions on my part I guided her into a hypnotic state.

> *Kate sensed herself to be about 20 years old, Native American, wearing a full skirt and with white moccasins on her feet. In wonder she said, "I behold a vast prairie, as far as the eye can see."*
>
> *Next Kate saw herself "walking around, sitting on the ground, telling stories to the children. They are laughing. My people are a happy people. They want no harm, just to be left alone and to live in peace."*

I moved her to "the next significant event that is affecting you now."

Kate:	I feel that no one will listen to me. I know of the pending doom, the devastation to come. I talk to my father; he is very old. He won't do anything. He hands me an eagle feather as a gift. I tell some women, but they don't listen either. They have no sense of the danger, as I do.
Janet:	Do you have family, a mate, or is there someone in your life?
Kate:	Yes, I have a mate, a lover. I am in his arms, embracing, such warmth, such love. He understands. He is a leader of sorts.

I again guided Kate forward in time.

| Kate: | I'm standing at a campfire watching the reflection of the fire glowing on people's faces. The men are sitting in a circle talking. My lover is there also. There is a split in the group. Some will fight, some will not. I'm angry. No! This is our land! We will fight! |

Continuing to move her ahead in time to the next event:

Kate: *My hands are burning. A man is holding them too tight. I*
           can't get away. I fight, kick. I want to scream. I'm being
           dragged away from camp. I want to bite his face off!

Kate was re-living the scene as her body moved and squirmed in
the hypnosis chair. She was angry, and crying hard.

Kate: *I'm on the ground, struggling. I'm too tired; I*
           can't resist any longer.

I guided her beyond that experience.

Kate: *I see him buttoning up his pants. I'm numb—just lying on*
           the ground. I sit on a rock, the wind is blowing my hair, it's
           cold.
                Now I'm back in the village, people are running,
           yelling, horses, confusion, heavy smell of smoke, swords
           being driven through bodies. I run and hide. I'm sobbing.

Tears ran down Kate's face as the stored emotions poured out of
her. I encouraged her tears.

Janet: *Let it all out, let it come, don't hold it back.*
Kate: *I come back...death all around. They might as well have*
           taken a sword and cut out my heart.

It took Kate a while to recuperate after the vivid experience that
she had under hypnosis. We talked about her impressions. "I saw
myself going off to commune with nature often," she said. "I seemed
to be a visionary of sorts. I saw things most people did not see—how
frustrating it was! My mate was Michael—he had visions, too."

My sense was that Kate had remembered a lifetime in the tribe
of Silver Eagle, even though her regression ended by her going back
to the village and finding its destruction. If her mate had been
Michael, however, this regression did not correspond to that of Roz,

when Michael was the son—a baby whose father was killed in a massacre.

Of course, almost every Indian tribe had ambushes, killings, and death as a part of their experience. Perhaps I had been mistaken and these people were simply friends with whom I enjoyed and felt a connection. It didn't matter; I certainly had no need to seek out "tribal members" for any purpose. If it were true that before the end of my life some would come to me for healing, it was not important whether I—or they—knew about that earlier lifetime. The importance would lie in the healing process.

So I did not spend any time trying to figure out whether or not my new friends had been present in the Silver Eagle lifetime. From a therapeutic standpoint, both of their regressions had given them information about beliefs, feelings, and issues at a very deep level, and healing had begun to occur. Releasing whatever anger and grief remained locked in the unconscious mind would free them both to deal more strongly with what was taking place currently, in the present life.

Michael

Soon after this time, Kate told me that Michael had been going through a difficult period and wanted to fly north to do some in-depth work with me. I doubled up on appointments for Michael during the time that he would be in town. Throughout these counseling sessions Michael would often separate himself in replying, "My head says...but my heart says..." I would remember this mannerism of speech several months later.

Our work together incorporated some hypnosis, including past-life regressions. We connected on several levels, and I recognized that as I challenged him he responded well and looked within for answers. Then he challenged me!

It happened this way. During one hypnosis session, he seemed to block the process of retrieving answers from the unconscious. This was okay. I knew that he was not able to retrieve that information yet. Then he laughed and said, "I just saw a falling star."

A Falling Star??? Michael did not know, nor did Roz or Kate, that what I recognized to be my soul name was Falling Star.

I decided to rationalize, to call it coincidence, and continue with the session. After all, anyone can see a falling star. I went on. Again, in checking out the willingness of his unconscious mind to get past-life or soul information related to a relationship he was in, Michael laughed again and said, "I see another one, a falling star!"

He did not know what he had said—but I did. His mind could not go there.... Perhaps I could get the information for Michael. Good grief! Could I do that? This was not anything that I did with clients, even very perceptive ones, like this one!

I decided to go with honesty. I told Michael that I had sensed things about him and that over the next few days I would see if anything came to me, and if so I'd tell him at our upcoming get-together with Kate and Roz. I explained to Michael that years ago I had done automatic typing, but I didn't do it anymore. I told him that I was in the process of breaking through some of my own unconscious blockages.

I shared that a few months earlier, while on vacation, I had given attention to two weeks of dream work. The insight from that experience helped me to understand that I was dealing with a very deep belief of, *"They don't want to hear what I have to say."* I realized that I had to move through that belief in order to do my work.

The young man across from me, it seemed, could see deep into a person's soul. Tears came to his eyes as he sat up and leaned forward in the chair, saying, "Janet, please, please, don't hide what you have to give. Yes, there are some people who may not be ready, but there are many others who do want, and need, to hear what you have to say." The teacher becomes the student becomes the teacher becomes the student.

Later I had a mini-seminar with Michael, Kate, and Roz that was fun and informal and enjoyable. Following a hand-drawn map I drove to Roz's apartment after work. Michael, who was staying there, prepared dinner—a delicious meal with tablecloth, linen napkins, flowers, candles, and wine. I had forgotten what such a treat could be like. My lifestyle had steered me toward pizza and too many fast-food meals.

Kate had made a decision to move to Florida, and she and Michael were going to find a place together. I could see that their energies would be good for each other at this point in time.

After my talk Michael said, "So, Janet, tell us what you *really* see with each of us." *He sure could put me on the spot.* Michael had seen that I sometimes stop myself in mid-thought, determining how ready a person is to hear me. Although I felt comfortable with whatever I told Kate and Michael that night, with Roz I was *extremely cautious* about what I said and how I said what I did. I still saw the powerful fear that blocked his creativity. I did not want to add to that fear, and I certainly did not want to suggest any of my own perceptions of what those fears might relate to. I do remember saying, "Roz, I know—I *know*—that in a regression, wherever you go, I am with you. You will not go further than I can go; I have proved that to myself."

I had handled Michael's prodding well, I thought. But once again I found that he was not going to let me off the hook. "Did you get any information on that relationship?" he asked. I felt as if my guides were getting *to* me through Michael. *Okay*, I thought, *I give up.* For the first time in many years, and in a group outside the Circle, I was going to channel. *Only with this group,* I thought, as I began to put myself into an altered state and gave what came to me in response to Michael's question.

Soon after this evening gathering, Michael returned to Florida and found an apartment for Kate and himself. Kate implemented the separation from her religious community and moved, taking a job setting up a new program for a clinic that worked with disadvantaged children.

DeLaine hated to see Kate and Michael leave. "It seems as if we just got re-acquainted," she said. From the day they met her, both Michael and Kate felt that they should be calling DeLaine "Mom."

Because DeLaine and I had found that our work complemented each other and clients often made faster progress when they came to both of us individually to work on mind *and* body, Roz began combining our approaches. When DeLaine saw pictures or got messages while working on his body, he came to me to find their meaning.

After one powerful session on a Friday evening, Roz spent the weekend in a dark depression. At his next appointment with me he said, "Janet, I demand—demand—that I go see whatever this problem is."

He was ready! "How horrible can it be?" he asked. He mentioned a few graphic possibilities. No matter what he had to look at, he was fed up with the headaches and feeling bad physically. He had spent years going to doctors and taking every test imaginable, only to be told that there was nothing wrong. What did he have to lose? "Let's do it," he said.

He faltered only slightly as I began his induction to the hypnotic state. Opening both eyes he said, "Now, you're sure you'll be with me wherever I go?"

"I'm sure," I said, and we moved to a very painful past-life trauma to assist him in his release of blockages to his seeing-vision and memories.

Having taken the inner step that was needed, Roz now felt ready to take action on the external plane. He located and rented a large studio space, something he had talked about for years, and for the first time in *eighteen* years he started painting.

I, as well, began taking external steps. In July of 1990 I moved to Owego, New York, without Scott. For quite a while I had felt like a little girl who was trying to grow up. *A little girl?* I was *forty-nine years old.* Scott had always taken care of me and I used to be quite content to have him do it. *Why couldn't I continue in that mode?* I knew it was my problem; I didn't seem to have the energy required to make the change *with* him. I felt disappointed with myself.

In spite of my "together" image externally, I did not feel very together inside. My world was changing, and I was scared. *No one* knew how scared I was.

Chapter VIII

Puzzle Pieces Fit Together: August 1990

Roz Begins to Paint

Michael and Kate had invited me to visit them in Florida, but such a trip seemed a luxury that I could not afford. Roz especially missed the company of his friends, so in a phone call with him I suggested that if some of us pooled our resources we could drive down together. I knew that DeLaine would love to go if she could get away. Marda had also mentioned a vacation, so I asked her if she would like to go, too.

Roz and DeLaine followed through. Roz found airline flights at a reasonable cost and DeLaine got Marda and me together to finalize plans. Marda had never even met Kate or Michael. I smiled and shook my head; it seemed that *the four of us were really going.*

It seemed appropriate to have Marda and Roz meet each other before our flight so we met for lunch, along with my son D. Scott (Scottie), who happened to be visiting from college. After lunch the three of us went to Roz's studio to see a painting he had just completed.

Roz unlocked a rather unnoticeable door beside a movie theater and led us up a narrow stairway to the third floor. "Up to heaven," he said. He unlocked another door to a huge area with an old wooden floor, high ceiling, and large windows that covered two outside walls and overlooked downtown Endicott, New York.

Souls Passing Over

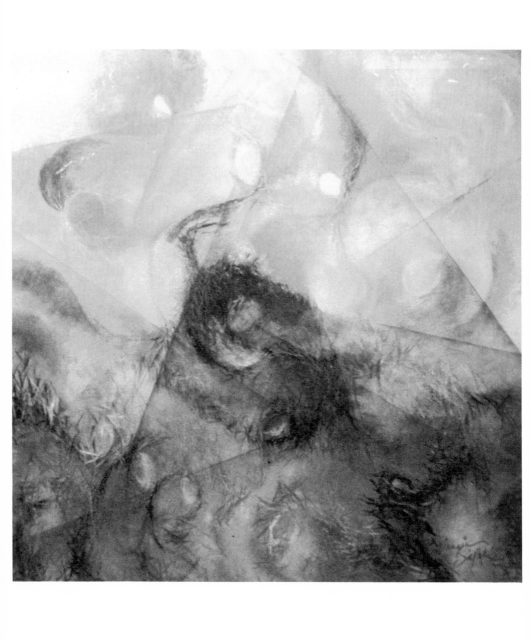

We pulled three chairs together and seated ourselves for the presentation. I was anxious to see the painting that he had begun. Roz walked up to a large frame that faced one wall and turned it around for us to see.

All of us stared in awe at the six-foot by six-foot canvas of what Roz described as "abstract expressionism." We were not artists, but we could not miss the power of what stood before us. We used different words—it looked like a depiction of "heaven and earth," "earth and sky," "hidden spirits," "struggle and peace."

"See these lines?" Roz asked as he pointed out the triangles in his painting. "I just added those lines last night—they're tepees. They'll be in each of the paintings in this show."

Tepees? I wondered. *Why would he put tepees into his paintings? His Indian regression had not been especially significant, compared to the more intense work that we had done together since that time. His choice did not make any sense to me, but I accepted his comment without further thought.*

As Scottie and I drove home, he expressed my sentiments: "Wow!" and said that he felt he had met Roz before, that he must have known Roz in a previous incarnation. Scottie's words were to prove prophetic, but not for some time to come.

Two weeks before we left, Marda came to me for a past-life regression. She had been physically ill and in distress mentally for a long time and decided she needed to learn what was causing her internal struggle. We did a powerful regression in which she found an original cause of many of her current-life issues.

Naples Vacation

On the day that our foursome left for Florida, Marda was still reeling from the emotional releases she'd had since that regression. "I feel like I have a hole in the center of me, so open and vulnerable," she said as she settled into her seat on the airplane. DeLaine, however, fairly burst with excitement. She was the one who had remembered a camera, film, snacks—still the mother.

As for me, I functioned on "automatic." Because of my move to Owego and all that had brought about my separating from Scott, I felt my energy to be totally depleted. On the other hand Roz looked forward to seeing his friends again. This included Heather Curtis, a student Roz had taught six years earlier who was currently living in Florida and had made contact with Kate and Michael.

Heather and Kate met us at the airport. Kate looked free and happy. Her usual neat attire now was lighter—white slacks and a pink and white print cotton blouse. Although none of us had met Heather before, we felt an immediate comfort and rapport with her. Her outgoing personality welcomed each of us warmly.

Heather was a woman in her late twenties with a large build. Bold in appearance and dress, she exuded a sense of strength, both physically and mentally. She had a beautiful smile, brown eyes, and a combination of youthfulness and a take-charge attitude complemented by a sense of humor. She dressed casually in flowered shorts, T-shirt, and sandals. Her medium-colored brown hair was styled short with the back in a perfect upsweep which added height to her five-foot eight-inch frame. It was Heather who took the wheel of a van to drive us to the town house where Kate and Michael lived.

Michael was watering the huge tropical plants on the patio as he waited for our arrival. If we had harbored any hesitation about all of us staying in one place, it disappeared when we walked through the door. The lovely and spacious surroundings delighted us. We were in the sun, we were on vacation, we were with friends. Marda, meeting Kate and then Michael for the first time, said, "I feel as if I've come home."

DeLaine and Heather took over most of the kitchen duty for us, preferring to handle grocery shopping and meal planning. DeLaine said, "I know that Heather was in that lifetime." Heather had always believed in reincarnation and felt an immediate closeness with us but did not want anything to do with having a regression!

That evening we meditated together. At a gem show I had been guided to pick up tiny "Apache tears" for everyone. I had not met Heather before, so I started counting out only enough for the people who had been clients and who held so much grief inside of them. As I counted, however, I felt a strong guidance to pick up one for

Heather. I gave one stone to each person around the circle and we began a meditation. At the conclusion I glanced at Michael. He sat across from me, smiling—our energy connection was strong. He had picked up on each person during the meditation and now shared what he had seen. With Marda, whom he had just met, he hesitated briefly and then said, "Passive, my ass!" Marda laughed; she knew exactly what he meant.

Our Naples visit included many delightful facets. Roz had taped a video recording of his studio and the painting he had done, so he could show them to his Florida friends and to DeLaine, who had not seen the painting. It was fun for all of us to share in this exciting step with Roz. All of us experienced healing—through our combined energy, through the beach and the sun, through deep conversations, through tears and through laughter, lots of laughter.

In packing for this trip I had brought eight pages that I had written for possible publication in a professional journal about the group regression I had done after the painting of Silver Eagle had arrived at my house. I had shared this writing with Kate following her Indian regression, and with Michael at the end of his visit north. Roz had never read it so I handed him the pages to read. He got comfortable with some pillows on the floor and I lay down on the couch nearby.

Roz made a couple of comments, curious at the story of how an artist's Indian painting could spur memories. He asked how much direction Scott had given to the artist, and I explained that he had given no direction other than to "paint an Indian." He had not specified male or female, he had not said "Chief," he had not indicated a tribe. "It is interesting that when Mrs. D. went to a library to research Indians," I commented, "the tribe that she selected was the Sioux." It had not been until recently that I had learned that the Oglala was connected with the Sioux.

Later, Roz and I discussed his own Indian regression. *In my mind, his didn't seem to fit with the experience of "our" tribe, because he (she) had lived to an old age and had not experienced a massacre. And, if Michael had been Running Deer, did Michael appear in that lifetime? And was Kate Michael's mate as she thought she had been? Yet Kate had memories of a massacre and had lived. No, the pieces did not fit together. Apparently we were talking about entirely different incarnations.*

Following an afternoon at the pool, DeLaine cornered Roz and began doing foot reflexology on him. From the time that she had first met Roz she had scolded him for not taking better care of his body, not eating well, and so on. "He won't listen," she said. "He didn't listen back in the tribe, either."

Michael's Healing

Meanwhile, Michael needed healing of his own. He found himself stalling when he came home from work. He had been feeling that he needed to look at something in his unconscious, and with this feeling came strong fear. For two days his emotions kept rising, but he promptly stuffed them back down so he could do his job.

After a swim to help him relax, Michael and I went upstairs. He lay on his bed and I began hypnotic induction. Michael moved into a deep trance state and found himself in a place of peace and love—another dimension. After a while I moved him to a different experience and he saw himself in an incarnation in a tropical place, perhaps Polynesia. We had examined that lifetime before, and I felt that his unconscious mind needed to recognize and remember those two times of peace and love before he could reach the past life that was affecting him negatively now.

> *Michael found himself alone...in buckskin or deerskin pants, bare chest...walking in the woods. He played with the small animals, squirrel and rabbits. He was about 16 years old, male, Native American.*

I had not expected an Indian incarnation. *Had he gone to the Silver Eagle tribe? Was he there?* If he had been there, his mind would likely have gone to the massacre. *No, this must be another Indian lifetime.*

As I moved him ahead in time, he saw himself with a young Indian girl who spent time with him: "She understands." I asked questions that determined that she and he were from the same tribe and she would occasionally go to find him. He spent time away from the tribe, alone. He often stood on the outskirts looking at the tepees of his people. He spoke of their love and acceptance of him. "Even in naming me, they understood who I was. They gave an appropriate name—Running Deer." Laughingly he said, "They knew I would always be running away."

I moved him to the next significant event—and suddenly the bottom seemed to fall out of his emotions. Michael's body lay on the bed as if frozen—arms and legs unmoving, yet emotion suddenly overtook his entire being. He started to sob and gasp for breath as he saw the pictures in his mind. I watched him carefully as he struggled, hardly saying anything other than, "No! Swords! They're cutting them up! Arms—Heads!" again gasping at the unimaginable horror of what he saw.

Neither of us had been prepared for or anticipated this! At any moment I expected him to scream out loudly in agony, and I wondered about the reaction of the others downstairs.

His head jerked to the side as if to try to stop the pictures, but they would not stop. "Take me out of here!" he panted, pleading.

His mind drew him in and out of the experience. I stayed with him in the movement. I assured him that I would take him out of it...yet I knew that he needed to see and remember enough so that he could fully experience the release that his soul-mind needed. I didn't want any error on my part here. I asked him more questions to learn where he was and what experience he was witnessing.

Michael was in the bushes, watching soldiers violently kill his people. He was frozen with fright and unimaginable terror before a soldier came up behind him...and Running Deer was decapitated.[2]

Michael was *re-living* this experience, and I, too, felt anxious to take him out of it. I directed him to let go of that scene and move away from the body and into spirit. As I continued to direct him away and into freedom, I realized that he was not letting go.

> *To my inquiries he explained that he was in spirit but could not leave. He felt locked to the earth with others who had passed over. "I cannot move; the Light welcomes us, but we can't go." I then sensed anger and rage rise up in Michael at what he continued to see in spirit. He and others witnessed and waited until the last torturous death of his people before slowly moving toward the Light, saying: "It will take time—much, much time."*

After Michael and I recuperated from the experience that had shaken both of us, we went downstairs for Chinese food—healing food, I call it. The others were anxious to hear about Michael's regression and where he had gone, if he were willing to share, but they could see that he did not feel ready to talk about it. The break of food, light talk, and laughter helped considerably to ground both of us again.

We were all sitting on the floor when Michael began to talk about where he had gone in his regression. Everyone sat in silence as he told of the memories that had burst forth from his unconscious mind. Tears flowed from Kate, DeLaine, Michael and me. Marda's sensitivity and empathy were strongly with us as she said, "I cried for two weeks before arriving—I think all my tears are gone."

With a group of people who have been clients and who have re-lived memories that I know are a part of their unconscious, it is automatically my nature to "monitor" the room. I watched Roz as Michael told about his regression. Roz began to cower into the corner where he was sitting. I started to move toward him, then decided against it so as not to interfere with the energy movement that was taking place. As Michael continued to share his memories of Running Deer, Roz pulled his knees up to his body and put his head down. Soon he began to sob. "I was in spirit on the other side," he said. "I was trying to pull all of you over. It was so horrible...you wouldn't come, you just stayed...I kept trying to pull you over to the other side!"

My God! That's what had happened! Roz's mate in that lifetime had been killed in a different tribal slaughter and Roz was taken in by our tribe. The son had been Michael—Running Deer. Running Deer grew up with our tribe and was mated to Kate. Roz passed over before the massacre. That's why his regression took him to a death at an old age. It hadn't made any sense before, but now the pieces fit. And...as an "angel" (the name he stumbled with when I asked his name) he helped pull us to the Light.

"It must have been mass confusion for the souls at that point of passing," I said. "Michael simply could not move. And I felt *such anger* rise up in him."

Michael walked upstairs and came back with a paper that he handed to me. He had written it five months previously:

ALL BUT MY ANGER

My senses are dulled—all but my anger.
Vague memories from scents inspire me to inquire,
But all I can grasp are distant glimpses.
I can't really remember—all but my anger.
How I wish to feel—all but my anger.
Warm gentle currents spark my curiosity.
Groping and flailing, I try to hold on,
But I can't really remember—all but my anger.
I wish to see life's visions—all but my anger.
The depths of colors before me reveal intangible flashes
Of time less turbulent than the present churnings.
But I can't really remember—all but my anger.

"Janet, this is an incredible story," Kate said. "I really think you should write about it. Think of how many people have stored memories about massacres and killing of Indian tribes in their consciousness. It would be so healing for people to read about our experiences."

"I don't know. I always thought Dot would write the story," I said, remembering back to the Circle meetings in our large house years ago. Each person in the room encouraged me to write it—*and* said they were willing to have their own names given.

"I'll illustrate it for you," Roz said.

Thinking of black ink sketches, I said,"It would be fantastic, Roz, to have you do illustrations. You actually have the pictures in your own memories." Roz's vision was still seeing pieces of the Indian incarnation as he talked to me.

"Maybe I can do a little sketching while I'm here next week," he said. "But after I get back, I'll first need to complete the paintings I've started in my studio."

This was our last evening together before Marda, DeLaine, and I flew home. Roz planned to stay a bit longer with his friends before school started. We shared with one another what the visit had meant to each of us and then stood up and took turns hugging one another in love and healing energy.

On the flight home the next day DeLaine sat between Marda and me, already feeling anxious about some tension she knew she would be facing. We talked about the fun vacation that we had had. When Marda mentioned Roz's paintings, DeLaine said, "I don't know why he said he couldn't do the illustrations and the painting at the same time. He's already doing it. He's painting the souls passing over."

My mouth dropped open, mirrored by Marda's: "DeLaine! You're right! That's what Roz is painting!" *He had started painting three months earlier—we had used the words heaven and hell, souls.... He had pointed out lines and said they were tepees that would be in all of the paintings for this show. It had made no sense at the time. He was painting what he saw!*

Chapter IX

Healing Art: September to December 1990

I felt too excited to wait for Roz to return from his vacation. I wrote to him in Florida, telling him what DeLaine had said and asking if he thought we were correct about the painting he had begun. He agreed.

A few days after our return I met Dot and Marilyn for lunch. I shared what had happened and told them that the others were encouraging me to write about the tribe. I was anxious to know if Dot still planned to write the story as fiction. She had not mentioned it for years but if she intended to tell the story, I would not begin. I would focus my energy on my business and the production of some tapes related to my research in weight control. Dot said, "No, I don't plan to write it. You are the one to tell the story; the Chief is the one to speak."

But I did not begin to write. Instead I followed through on the cassette tape project, which consumed most of my time and energy. Meanwhile, many of us began to experience change and healing in unexpected ways.

Roz Paints the Souls Passing Over

Roz continued to paint. "It's like it's just coming right out of me!" he exclaimed. He had finished the lower half of the second painting before our trip to Florida. Roz described this painting as "more intense." Intense was hardly the word for it, as I saw it before its completion. "I had too much red in it," Roz said. "I had to wipe off the red, there was so much that I had put on the canvas."

This second painting, as the first, seemed to depict souls passing over. This one, however, showed the emotion of confusion and pain. In the lower left-hand corner was a face that appeared to be clearer than the others. I said, "Roz, you've painted the face of Silver Eagle."

"I have? Do you think so?" he asked. "I don't know. All I'm painting is what comes to me." Even though Roz's work was abstract and not realistic like the painting of Silver Eagle that hung in my apartment, he had captured the same facial structure and features.

Roz had never seen the painting of Silver Eagle done by Mrs. D., so I invited Marda, DeLaine and him over for pizza. He brought the video of his paintings—the most recent one now added—to show the others. When DeLaine saw the figure on Roz's painting she gasped, "It's Silver Eagle!" Marda agreed with her, and Roz sat quite still in amazement. With the video in a hold position on Roz's work, I turned my face back and forth between the television set and the painting on my wall. Roz had indeed painted the same nose, the same close-set eyes, the same chin.

The face of Silver Eagle was not the only one that would appear in Roz's work. He phoned a few days later after a full day at his studio. "Janet," he said, "there is this one face that really bothers me. It's a little girl, and she seems to be looking for someone." *I knew that I had been the little girl, but for now I didn't comment. I preferred to ignore this thought until I saw his painting.*

By the time I visited the studio, Roz had completed three panels, the total size about six feet tall by eighteen feet wide. His images were powerful. "The little girl is in this painting, too," Roz said. "She bothers me so much."

I sat back and stared at the paintings—*but I could not find this face of the little girl.* Roz walked up to the abstract depiction of the souls at the time of the massacre. He pointed out the face, eyes, direction in which she was looking—toward the male face in the lower left corner, the one that we had determined to be Silver Eagle—*and still I could not see her. It was as though my mind had*

Chaos In the Transition

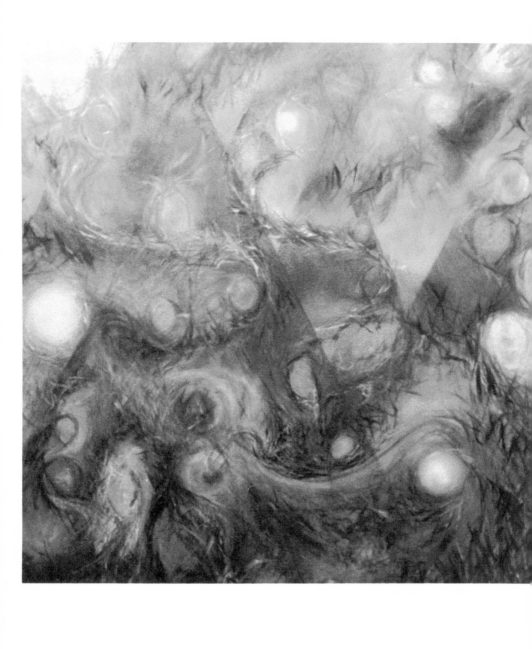

Golden Winged Hawk Helps the Soul

blocked this memory. I shook my head, quite aware of my confusion. *Perhaps I expected this face to be clearer—I observed my mind fighting a memory, one that I had not yet chosen to see more clearly.*

I was not the only one as yet unable or unwilling to look more deeply. Many of us began to experience changes and healings in unexpected ways. A year earlier the anger that DeLaine had stored since childhood had reached a point where it could no longer be contained. She had shocked even herself with eruptions that had burst forth at her husband. Now, after her return from Florida, it became her husband's turn to vent stored emotion, something we had learned must be released for one's healing. As the recipient of his anger, DeLaine changed from an independent woman and healer to a wife and mother who responded only to her family and seldom left the house. We were astonished at her reaction to what was taking place.

Marda also went through a time of painful transformation. As a fiftieth birthday gift to herself, Marda had braces put on her teeth to correct her bite and eliminate possible problems in the future. She could not know that this choice would begin a time of physical and mental suffering that would puzzle all of us. Her persistent pain baffled the dentists, and months would pass before she would know the actual cause of her suffering.

On other fronts it seemed as if things had speeded up, with bits and pieces of information coming to us, often unexpectedly. One day I listened to a new client who had come seeking help for depression. As she sat across from me, talking about how she hated every cell of her body, *I suddenly knew that she had been a soldier—a leader in the massacre of our tribe. I found myself in two places—calmly listening and not changing the expression on my face, while at the same time recognizing a soldier who had been instrumental in our massacre.* It was an erie experience.

This client was, without doubt, one of the most negative people I had ever met. Even though she believed in past lives I neither encouraged nor attempted hypnosis with her. She said that her unconscious held too much self-hate to open her memory just at this point. I agreed with her. *I did not mention my own perceptions of the Indian life.* She wanted me to agree that I could not help her, so I agreed. When I arrived home that evening I put her into my "prayer box" and did a meditation, asking that White Light and healing energy fill her soul.

Karen

Another woman called to make an appointment for counseling, saying that she wanted to open more to her creativity. She said that Roz Salati recommended that she contact me. This woman explained that she had seen Roz's paintings and had felt overwhelmed. In discussion he had said, "What you see here would not have been possible if it hadn't been for Janet Cunningham." We made an appointment. Her name was Karen Kim.

Karen hurried into my office and we introduced ourselves as she sat down. I looked at a lovely lady who had startling big blue eyes. She was well dressed in an artsy style with loose clothing and large quality jewelry. Her long, light brown hair flowed freely with stylish curl.

Karen told me about her busy life. She owned and operated a craft gallery in a nearby town. Her gallery carried one-of-a-kind items for sale, including quality Native American art, sculpture, pottery, jewelry, and weavings. During a counseling session I sometimes open my receptors to "sense" from the client as he or she is talking. As she continued to talk about her family and childhood, I found myself being more open, and I almost interrupted her as I said, "I sense such sadness from you."

Immediately tears welled up in her eyes as she replied, "Yes, I know, and I don't know why! I have a pretty good life."

We continued our discussion as I explained the process of regression and generally how I work. She made an appointment to return. As she left I found myself saying, "Karen, every once in a while I'm particularly glad to see a person walk through this door—I'm really glad you came."

Why in the world did I say that! I'm happy to see every client walk through the door—why was I so glad to have Karen come to me? I puzzled over this comment that I had never made to a client before.

Suddenly came a flash of intuition: Karen had been in the tribe. *Come on, Janet, you're getting carried away*, I thought, and never mentioned it to anyone.

Karen's regression seemed to be intertwined with memories, possibly of more than one Indian incarnation, and *very strong fear* that interfered with her clear perception. She moved to a lifetime where she saw herself as white[3] and married to a Native American.

> *When her husband and others were killed, she and the other women escaped into the woods, but she could not go on with them. To help insure the survival of her infant son, on the advice of her husband's mother she handed the baby to her...and never saw the child again. With this realization, Karen burst into tears.*
>
> *Throughout this hypnosis session she smelled smoke and felt a burning sensation and dryness in her nose and throat.*

After she emerged from the regression we talked about it. She wondered if she had made it all up. "That's a common feeling," I told her. "What do you think?"

"If it weren't for the emotion I would say that I did make it all up—I didn't make that up! And it does explain the strong connection I have felt with the American Indian ever since I was a child." She talked of the many feelings and connections that her regression helped her to understand, feelings related to the military, to Indians, even to her craft gallery that she wanted to *fill* with Native American art but balanced with other saleable art pieces.

Above all, she had always wanted an Indian baby cover-board—and had recently priced one for the store for several thousand dollars. "I told the woman who works with me, "I just have to have a coverboard." It has almost been an obsession."

The regression had gone well, though Karen's conscious mind had evaluated and fought during the process. She had retrieved very little information about that lifetime but enough to hit the emotion and recognize its effects. That was most important. *No, I did not feel that this had been the Oglala tribe. I forgot about it.*

Karen went to see Roz the next day, specifically to ask him if during regression one might feel that he or she has made it all up. "Yes, I did feel that way, especially the first time," Roz replied.

Again Karen spent time with Roz' paintings and called me a week later saying, "I have been in such a turmoil since I saw you; I need to come in again."

At our next session Karen returned to the same lifetime and received more information, but we both wondered if deep fear and trauma had interfered with the process. Once more she smelled smoke and felt a dryness in her nose and throat. Again I surprised myself with the openness with which I talked to Karen at only our second meeting. I mentioned my sister-in-law Sara's psychic abilities and that Sara would be visiting the following weekend. Sara planned to attend a wedding and time would be limited, but I felt that Karen would benefit from a reading if she were interested. The regressions, I recognized, were valuable, but I sensed that Karen's unconscious mind held some deep trauma that could not yet be released in that manner. She eagerly said yes to a reading and asked me to call if one could be arranged.

It was a whirlwind weekend. My older son, Dan, flew in to be in his friend Brian Cochrane's wedding. Since I expected Sara at my house, Dot met Dan at the airport. In fact, Dot had wanted to spend some time with Dan. Members of our "extended Circle" continued to use their overlapping abilities to help one another's healing. Dot and my older son Dan had assisted each other over the years.

Sara was one of those who attended the wedding. She and I did not get together often, so we enjoyed our time to talk as we rushed between appointments. We did not mention the Silver Eagle tribe, however, and I gave her no information about the new people she would meet that day. I made tea and watched as Sara gave a reading to one of my clients. The reading completed, we scurried out to buy a wedding gift, then drove the twenty minutes to meet Karen at the craft gallery.

The three of us went out for coffee. Sara had just sat down across from Karen in the booth when she said softly, "Janet, Karen was in the massacre." Tears came to my eyes at this confirmation of what I knew to be true. Sara continued, "She was tortured badly...by fire."

Karen asked the waitress for extra paper napkins. It looked as if we were going to need them. We learned that in the Indian life Karen had one child, who in the present lifetime is Ginger Zack, Sara's daughter. Sara's reading then took a lighter tone, and she introduced Karen to two strong male Indian guides.

Our next step was a visit to Roz's studio where Sara and my son Dan met Roz for the first time. Dan was twenty-five years old, six feet tall with thinning light brown hair. His strong energy moves out from him in a natural and comfortable manner. He has a casual, flowing personality with a pleasant disposition and sense of humor and a laugh that carries people with him.

I watched the eyes of the people around the room as they gazed at Roz's paintings. Dan moved easily into an altered state of consciousness. He had to force himself to "stay grounded" while staring at the depiction of souls passing. Roz had just started work on a painting of the face of Silver Eagle, Dot could not take her eyes from it.

Sara was amazed at what she was seeing. She told Roz that he had such compassion for Silver Eagle because he had been a chief in another very early American Indian tribe. At that earlier time, his tribe members had been concerned with basic survival, with food and shelter. According to Sara, Roz had reincarnated as a "worker," a woman, who intended to assist in the passing of souls to the Light...*and in his present life* he had returned to assist in the healing of these souls through his art.

Upon learning that Karen had been in the tribe, Roz said to me, "Now Janet, isn't this getting carried away? Karen comes to see my paintings, you just met her, and now she is in the tribe. Is everyone we meet from the tribe?"

I understood perfectly well Roz's questioning; I continued to question it, also. Nevertheless, I found myself smiling as I said, "Let me assure you, Roz, that I have had plenty of clients who were not in that lifetime. And I have many friends who were not in the tribe." By that time I had done over a thousand individual past-life regressions. By the time I would write about the tribe, only twenty of those individual sessions plus one group regression would include the Silver Eagle tribe.

I still had not taken any steps toward writing about the tribe. Instead, I was working on cassette tapes that I was preparing for my business. Roz was designing a cover for them, in preparation for my business. He asked me to meet him at work in the art rooms of the high school to finalize his drawing for me to take to the printer.

As I drove to Endicott I found myself taking deep breaths; I could not seem to get air into my lungs. The experience was an unusual one for me, though I had seen Dan do the same thing on occasion—a need to make conscious effort to get air. I was quite aware that I had kept the Life Force—air, prana, chi, oxygen—limited in my physical body, not by breathing in a shallow manner, but rather breathing only enough—only enough. So I felt puzzled and surprised at my own body reaction as I drove to meet Roz—at the effort I needed to make just to get air into my lungs.

After working on the art design, Roz and I got a bite to eat and visited his studio. He had installed some new lighting and was anxious to show me the paintings under better lights.

Roz Paints the Agony of Silver Eagle

When I entered the studio, the canvas of the face of Silver Eagle on the easel made me do a 180-degree turn. My mouth opened, and I felt suspended for moments in time. Roz had captured the agony and tortured soul of the man. I sat spellbound.

Roz pulled up a chair for me to sit down, as he said, "This is just the undercoat."

Just the undercoat? I thought. *Just the undercoat? Good God!*

He went on to comment on the cheekbone, changes that would come in the nose and skin. He pulled up a chair beside me as he took a breath and said, "Do you know anything about how he died? I feel that I need to know. I sat here last night, thinking that it might come to me. I feel like I might put something into his eyes, but I don't know what yet."

Silver Eagle

I told Roz what I knew, that Silver Eagle had died last, after being kept alive and forced to see the last of his people killed. I said that I knew DeLaine, Margaret and I had been present at the end and that I had died immediately before him. "I know that his face was the last one that I saw before passing over," I said. I continued to stare at the painting on canvas before me. My eyes remained glued to the figure, as if my mind had begun to bring memory forward, and strongly resisted at the same time. "He watched me killed right before his death," I added.

We continued our discussion as I commented on Michael's regression and what he had seen. "I know that the Chief was dismembered," Roz said as he pondered the canvas.

"Your paintings are a part of my healing process, Roz," I told him. "I'm not sure that I'm able to see what happened. Something deep inside me just cannot believe that human beings could do such things."

Roz walked over to the lighting. As he turned the dimmer switch down, I could not believe my eyes! It looked as if he had painted the souls in iridescent paint! The Light Beings or circles on the canvas shone as if they had just been released from hell.

"Look at this," Roz exclaimed. "Isn't it eerie?"

"Good heavens, I don't believe this! Did you know what you were doing?" I burst out, already knowing the answer. No, he had not even discovered it until the new lighting had been mounted just a few days earlier.

That night as I drifted off to sleep I thought, *I need to see more clearly.* I was not referring to any past life—I meant the present. Nevertheless, I remembered that thought hours later.

From a deep sleep I woke at 2:30 in the morning. Deciding to rest, I curled into a ball and purposely moved my mind to pleasant thoughts. But Roz's painting kept entering my vision. Again I reviewed what I knew about the end of that life for members of the tribe...*and I wondered what had actually happened to me. Would I ever know? Did I have to know?*

My mind moved to my body, and I thought about my left hand. For the past two weeks I had awakened with my left hand numb. My

logical mind searched: *Was I sleeping on it? No, that was not the case.*
My hand seemed to be fine during the day and I never thought about
it, other than when I woke to find it numb. *Did something happen to
my hand? I remembered that from childhood to the time I was married,
I would awake from sleep with both of my hands above my head,
crossed at the wrists, as if bound and hanging. Even now, anytime that
I slept alone, without Scott, I would wake up in that position.*

What happened at the end for Silver Eagle and me? I wondered as
I continued a mental search of my body for cell-memory clues. I
remembered that during bodywork a psychic friend in trance had
given DeLaine instructions to "sew her back together. Janet has
separated herself." Two years had passed with no apparent effect;
*perhaps I was the one who had to "repair" myself. Perhaps I had to
remember and be willing to "reconnect" myself in consciousness.* I
recognized a truth in what had been channeled. People talked of
being centered, referring to the solar plexus; my own centering came
closer to the head area. My intuition was mental while other people
had actual gut reactions or signals in the solar plexus. That had
seldom been my experience. My "gut reactions" or "knowing" came
from an area well above the heart center. *Had I died by being cut
across my body...and did my father see it happen?*

At that point I knew that upon my death Silver Eagle's spirit had
released from his body...with a soul scream.

I tossed and turned for two hours. I got out of bed, put some
milk and honey into a pan to warm, and turned on the computer to
write. It was 4:30 A.M.

I wrote about my thoughts during the night related to the end of
Silver Eagle's life. I started sneezing. *I can't get a cold now, I com-
manded. I start production on my tapes today. My voice needs to be
clear; I can get a cold after the tapes are recorded.* As I had done many
times, I used my mind to control my body. *Would that method still
work?* I hoped so—arrangements had been made to record over the
next three days. I couldn't come down with a cold now. I remembered
once when Elaine had a long-lasting cold and said to me, "It's as if
my body is crying and my mind can't let it happen." Something inside
of me feared that if I reached those tears, my tears, I would never be
able to stop them.

Planning a Celebration

Michael would be coming north to spend the holidays with his family. In a phone call I asked him when his flight would be and he said he had not yet made arrangements, "although December 21st sticks in my mind—I don't know why."

"You don't know why December 21st is important?" I asked.

"No, I don't..." Then he suddenly remembered, "Oh, that's when I met you last year—it's your birthday."

A few weeks later I felt guided to send a letter to a "certain tribe of friends," inviting them to a celebration on December 21st. I explained in my note that it would be a gathering for only those people who had lived in the Native American tribe with Silver Eagle and that they might enjoy meeting some people whom they had not seen in a very long time. I asked, also, if anyone had an individual regression from years earlier that had been taped, because I would appreciate borrowing it to trigger my memory.

Robert responded to my request but not in a way that I expected. He said that he had listened to his regressions and that it had been an emotional experience for him. "I've decided that I don't want to release the tapes," he said.

"Okay, I'd still like to meet with you sometime to check out your memories," I replied, and he agreed. At the time of his regressions he hadn't shed a tear—it had taken four years for him to be able to reach the emotion of that life.

Michael had been corresponding with me weekly by mail since our work together and our connection had grown stronger. Michael's psychic abilities had opened after his powerful regression. As with most of the people with whom I had worked, when energy blockages are released, more abilities and talents begin to flow. Sometimes, though he was several hundred miles away, Michael was as clear on things that were happening among our group as we were.

His sensitivity grew powerful; he could pick up on another person's energy and *feel* what was happening with them. We discussed this in letters. We discussed soul growth and love and relationships. To my plea for help he composed what I called "Falling Star music" as background to my voice for a stress-reduction tape that I had made. He also had a good singing voice; Michael was loaded with creativity. However, this exceptionally talented young man wanted and needed more space from people than most require.

One evening he called and in a lengthy discussion said, "Janet, you can't do the writing there. Your business and obligations keep you in the left-brain too much. You need to be free to do the writing. And you need to reach your own memories of the Silver Eagle tribe. You need to be in a safe place, a soft space, to remember. Will you come to Naples?"

I told him that I would think about it. I knew that he was right. I had to remember...and I didn't know how I was going to do it. I was also fearful of re-living the experience that I had guided so many others through.

As if reading my mind Michael said softly, "Janet, they will not get to you now. It's okay...it's okay." Tears welled up in my eyes at the sensitivity of my telephone companion.

Marda also called me and said, "Janet, I think that my nephew, Timothy, is supposed to be at the party." With the openings to that memory becoming clearer among us, I trusted Marda but said that I would like to "check it out." She heartily agreed. I had met Timothy years earlier when we had held Circle meditations at Marda's house; I felt a real connection to him then.

I started to ask DeLaine or Dot but decided against it. It was time for me to trust my own knowing. I went into an altered state and received the following:

> *You ask of one called Timothy. In the Silver Eagle tribe, yes, there were two other family members. The young man, Timothy, was a child friend to Running Deer. He looked up to Running Deer as a warrior. Running Deer ran from his warrior-heart...knowing his strength and seeing the visions to come. By warrior-heart I refer to the heart of the protector, the strong of the tribe, the fighters and hunters. Running Deer/Michael is a fighter....although he might not view himself in that way. It is his fighting quality, among other abilities, that benefits my daughter at this time.*

I called Marda to ask if what I had received felt right to her and she said, "Absolutely."

DeLaine's home situation was steadily growing more tense. She had long felt that her husband blamed her for the death of their oldest daughter, Lynette, though he denied it. There were times when she would call Marda or me to talk, and the tone and content of the conversation switched in mid-stream when her husband walked through the door. The woman who had always spoken to others about doing what they needed for their peace and health was not doing this for herself. All that we could do was stand back and let DeLaine walk through her own lessons and be there to give our support and love.

Marda, however, found herself growing more and more frustrated with DeLaine. "She doesn't listen to what I say, Janet. It's like she ignores me when I talk. It makes me angry and I don't understand why it's bothering me so. I know that DeLaine has to go through this. I know that she is not able to act for herself now and that she simply needs to learn something. But I get so aggravated with her! You seem to be handling it better than I am—I get so angry."

Several weeks later, while Marda drove home from Roz's studio she started sobbing. She had had a spontaneous regression while driving and remembered that back in the tribe White Fawn (DeLaine) had refused to listen to her. As Little Feather, Marda had been out playing alone when she saw a soldier sneaking around. She ran back to the village excitedly to tell White Fawn. But White Fawn had been so busy working and caring for other children that she ignored Little Feather, thinking that the soldier had been something from the child's imaginings.

"No wonder I have felt so angry at DeLaine for not listening," she said. "She didn't listen then, either. The next time that I went out alone, I never came back."

About this time a phone call from Roz stunned me. "Oh, Janet," he said softly, *"The Grandfathers said that you would be the next Chief. They were seeing into the future—they saw you bringing the tribe together in this lifetime."*

Meanwhile, Roz asked me to come to the studio to see the painting of Silver Eagle that he had completed. "I think it's my finest work," he said. I sat down and waited while he set the lights and turned the canvas around. I sat there speechless. He had captured the end. I sat in silence for a long time, and tears came to my eyes. Roz played music in the background—I didn't even try to talk. With the massive panels that he had painted I had expressed enthusiasm and excitement, but with this one I remained speechless. Finally I turned to him and said, "Roz...I simply don't have any words...This painting is incredible; there are no words that adequately express what this says to me."

As the party drew nearer I began to wonder if I'd lost my mind. Having a party to celebrate our return? What if it's not real? Maybe none of it happened. Maybe we've just fed each other's delusions. I sat down and made a list of people who knew that they had been in that lifetime—some people who had never met—people who were much more trusting of their memories than I was of mine. I listed twenty-three people—and more would come!

Chapter X

The Celebration: December 21, 1990

It was December 21st and I had decorated my apartment with a Christmas tree covered with homemade ornaments. The maple dining table and marble-top coffee table held centerpieces of pine and candles. I lit all the candles and enjoyed the soft glow and holiday spirit. This was to be perhaps the most unusual party that any of us had ever attended—a party to celebrate our return, the return of a group of people who held memories of a past life together and had returned for healing.

I had taken my time getting ready, putting on a silk two-piece tie-dyed dress with beautiful shades of orchid and blue. Knee-length burgundy boots complemented my outfit. Looking out at the fog, I wondered about those traveling by car and plane and hoped that no one would have trouble getting to my place.

This was also my birthday. Michael had written that he would be happy to "celebrate the reincarnation of Falling Star." He and Kate were flying to upstate New York from Florida.

And it was the winter solstice. Joyce, my astrologer friend, said that both my chart and the location of this gathering indicated "ancient knowledge brought to the earth."

My thoughts were interrupted by the first arrivals, Marda and Timothy, her nephew, whom I had not seen for several years. I welcomed having a few minutes to get reacquainted with Timothy. I remembered his gentleness and friendly manner. He was 22 years old, about five feet eight, with light blond hair and piercing blue eyes. He gave me a strong hug. I usually listen carefully to what a person says, because sometimes the words come out of the unconscious. In his first few statements Timothy said, "We have one year." *Did he mean that we had one year before we all began to move in different directions? My instincts said yes.*

More people arrived soon afterward, and the apartment filled with some of my closest and dearest friends, along with my husband, and my younger son, Scottie. Several attending had been close friends of each other for five years or longer, while some were meeting tonight for the first time. Excitement and laughter and hugs spread all around me as I watched friends and strangers who, though they had not seen each other before, did not seem to be strangers at all.

An outside observer would have seen a very "normal-looking" group of men and women, ranging in age from 22 to 63. But anyone who listened more closely to their conversations could hear a light humor in introductions of one another and explanations of relationships in that past incarnation.

"This is so confusing," Karen said, laughing. "I have enough trouble remembering names of this life." Karen was very new to this group and told me later that she expected to feel out of place. It didn't happen. Not only did she feel "that I belonged," she also felt that she was with family. She and Deb hit it off at once and compared notes on their teen daughters. Karen had also been a nurse and worked at the same hospital where Deb was now employed.

Marda had been anxious for Timothy to meet Michael and Roz. Timothy shook hands with Michael and then hugged him, unexpectedly bursting into tears. I walked over and put my arms around both of them. Everyone understood the soul connection that had just taken place.

Joyce, our astrologer, had a great time running around collecting birth dates and birth locations. It felt good to have both Scott and my son Scottie at the Celebration. Scottie had had minor surgery on his foot before driving in for the holidays.

While I talked with Michael I saw his attention suddenly move. "Where did you just go?" I asked.

"My foot is hurting. I think I'm picking up on someone else's pain," he said.

I led him to where Scottie was standing, and said, "Scottie, I think Michael is picking up on your pain. Is your foot hurting?"

"Oh yes, it was," he said, "but I shut the pain off at the calf so I wouldn't feel it."

We laughed—Scottie had shut off the pain with his mind, and Michael had picked up the energy. "He is certainly *your* son!" Michael exclaimed.

I asked Michael if he could get Scottie's name from that life. I assumed that Scottie had been an infant. Michael replied, "I can see Scottie. He was older, he wasn't a child. No, I don't know his name. I keep sensing horses around him."

After sufficient social time around a couple of food-laden tables, I called everyone to gather into one large circle. Changing my diet soda to a glass of white wine as I entered the living room, I lifted my glass:

> *As many of you know, sometimes I do or say things that seem to come out of my own inner guidance or from an outer direction. That is what happened when I felt guided to call us together to celebrate tonight. I know each of you deeply in many ways...many ways...and I toast you for having the guts to return, the wisdom to return, and the love to return. I celebrate with you, and I thank you for coming back with me.*

Deb Nelsen always celebrates the winter solstice with an Indian ritual, and I invited her to do that if she desired. I knew that a few who were present might be surprised at the Indian-connectedness to ritual that is so much a part of Deb's life today, even though she is a "non-typical" white American.

The group fell silent as Deb moved into the center of the circle of people sitting on chairs, couches, and on the floor around my living room. She took out the wing of a Great Horned Owl and lit sage in an abalone shell that she had brought with her. She moved around the circle as participants cleansed any negative energy from their auras, and then Deb offered the gift to the four directions. Her long black hair hung straight down her back to her waist. She kneeled in the center and with a strong and melodious voice began to chant.

Deb was more connected to Indian ritual than anyone else in the room. Privately she had followed practices of Native Americans since long before I had met her; she often attended Sun Bear's gatherings when they were held in the Northeast. I smiled internally, wondering about the thoughts of several who were meeting her for the first time tonight who would be surprised at how "Indian" she appeared. At the conclusion she looked at me and I thanked her for sharing with us.

The Tribe Members Introduce Themselves

I then invited everyone to introduce him/herself to the group as a whole and to say a few words about memories of that tribal lifetime or how each happened to be in attendance at this party. I started with the person to my right, my son Scottie. Scottie had driven in from college that evening. He had just completed final exams and was looking forward to a holiday period of relaxation. With a mother's pride I looked at his handsome six-foot-one frame sitting on the floor beside me. Even more evident to me, and to others, was the quiet strength that Scottie displayed for his 22 years.

> *"Well, I'm here because my mom is the one who does all of this weird stuff,"* he joked, and then became more serious. *"I think I'm here for the healing that is needed after a stressful time at college. I just finished my bachelor's degree last week."*

Because Scottie had not referred to the Indian incarnation I added, "All that we know at this point is that Scottie was in that lifetime, so perhaps information can come from someone tonight."

I looked to Joyce to speak next. Although she was the oldest one in our group, Joyce certainly did not look or act older than the others. On many occasions some of us had been known to say, "I'd sure like to look like Joyce when I'm her age." Not only her looks, but also her attitude is youthful, and she was in especially good spirits on this evening.

I met this group of people through Janet several years ago. When I first went to their meditation circle I wondered, Are they kidding? ...and I began to realize, No, they aren't kidding! I'm an astrologer, and I'm curious about everyone's charts, so I took down their birthdays and I was amazed at the charts of these people. They all had past-life ties that were indicated in their charts...and they connected with mine, too. This is a group of healers who have come back for the New Age. As far as my own memories of that life, I don't have a lot, other than having been one of a small group in the tribe that went away to a cave to die.

The next person to speak was Kate Paul. Most of the people present had never met Kate, who had left her religious community only nine months earlier. Kate's beautiful silver-grey hair enhanced her attractive tall, slim appearance.

My name is Kate Paul and I live in Naples, Florida, having moved there nine months ago after leaving the convent of which I had been a part for 28 years. People probably thought it strange for me to go to Florida and live with Michael, whom I'd known for several years, but it seemed like the right thing to do. I met Michael through Roz, and the three of us have been very special friends. Our friendship has increased during the last couple of years.

I went to Janet for counseling and eventually had a regression to the Indian lifetime that we refer to. In that life Michael was my mate, and DeLaine took care of me like a mother. Recently in Florida I met the woman who had been my mother in that life. It was a very powerful experience. My name was Little Star. I remember coming back to the village and seeing the burning tepees and destruction.

That regression helped to explain my strong connection to the Indian people in my current life and my desire to help them. I worked at the Sioux Indian reservation in North Dakota for three years. After my regression I learned that the tribe that we were a part of was the Oglala, which is connected to the Lakota-Sioux.

Kate glanced at the painting of Silver Eagle that Mrs. D. had done. It hung on my living room wall. She continued:

When I went to Janet's office for my regression, I wore around my neck a beaded necklace that the children had given me when I left. In the center of the necklace was a silver eagle.

Marda spoke next. At first meeting, Marda might appear more to be the former nun than Kate. Her passive way and easy mannerisms continued to mask the strong person inside. The braces on her teeth had given her terrible problems for months, and again and again she drew forth strength in her four-foot eleven-inch body and continued to tough it out.

About seven years ago I got a group of women together to meet once a week at my house. I thought of it as a meditation group or a prayer circle. I named it the Circle of Love. This is the result of that beginning!

In the tribe I was a young girl, about 13 years old at the time of the massacre. Most of my memories about that lifetime are of the beauty of the land and the spirit of the people. I know that my parents had died and that DeLaine helped raise me. Janet and I were playmates and like sisters. I died early, before the worst of the massacre took place. My name was Little Feather.

As each person spoke about memories, a hush and attentiveness filled the room. There was a respect and understanding as each listened to the subdued memories being recalled.

Michael was now 30. He had purposely darkened his already dark skin in the Florida sun so he wouldn't "fade" while spending a week in New York. He had squeezed his slim body between Marda and DeLaine on the small Victorian settee.

My name was Running Deer, for those of you who don't already know, because I tended to run away from things. I liked to play in the woods with the small animals. I've written some poetry about that lifetime. Kate will share a few of my poems later. In my regression...

Michael took a deep breath to control the emotion that rose automatically. Others in the room seemed to take that same deep breath with him. Several reached for tissue boxes that I had placed around the circle.

...I was in the woods and witnessed the massacre taking place before I was beheaded.

Eyes filled with tears. Michael did not try to continue but instead handed the tissue box to DeLaine, laughingly saying, "Here, Mom." DeLaine pulled a couple of tissues out of the box, laughing.

I was everybody's mom!

When DeLaine laughs, everyone laughs with her, infected by the honest and hearty laugh that springs up from inside her. Many in the room still felt "mothered" by DeLaine, who commonly would shake her finger, scolding any one of us for not eating enough, or for the kinds of foods we were eating, or for our lack of exercise or rest. DeLaine's fire energy was now being tested by life. She had not had an easy time for the past several months, and we were happy to have her in our midst.

I was one of Silver Eagle's mates. My name was White Fawn. My memories are of always cooking and taking care of the children. It seems like that's what I've always done—cooking and taking care of children. It wasn't until recently in a regression with Janet that I realized that I still carried a lot of anger toward Silver Eagle for what happened.

Timothy's turn came next. He was a senior in college, and his presence was new to most of the people in the room.

>*My name is Timothy Gardner and I'm Marda's nephew. I'm here because of several strange and unusual circumstances that led up to my becoming aware that I was a part of this tribe. I'm going to have a regression with Janet tomorrow, so I don't know much about who I was or what my name was. If anyone else knows I'd appreciate your telling me. I am familiar with a few of you through the meditation circle that met in Marda's house. Tonight I feel like I've come home to the people I've searched for all my life.*

The tissue box had become the "talking stick," an Indian symbol of authority to speak in the circle. Timothy passed the tissues to Roz, and Karen and I jokingly reached for another box, saying that we needed one between us as he spoke. Roz smiled and thoughtfully took the box.

During the past year I had watched as Roz had taken on more of an "artist image," with pony tail and a pierced ear. These symbols served as an external indication of the internal freedom that he had gained. He wore an Indian Sioux neckpiece of hairbone, a gift from Karen.

>*My name is Orazio Salati, and people call me Roz. I was born in Italy and came to this country when I was seven years old. I am an artist. I teach art—drawing, sculpturing, design, jewelry, pottery, and weaving. Some of my pieces in the past have been Native American arts in pottery and weaving. Michael was a student of mine years ago and introduced me to Kate, who has been a friend for 13 years. I was invited to the Sioux reservation as a visiting artist.*
>
>*I met Janet on this date—December 21—just one year ago. For 16 years I had had difficulty with headaches and seeing things that I didn't understand; Janet had been recommended by someone who had gone to her. I told Kate and Michael that when I heard her voice, I would know whether or not to make*

the appointment. I talked to Janet over the phone, made an appointment, and then turned to Michael and Kate and said, "She's the one." But when I went for my appointment I took Michael and Kate with me for that first regression, which was to my childhood.

"Wasn't your name Golden Chicken?" Michael joked as we all laughed. "Oh, hawk—it was hawk."

We had all grown accustomed to moving rapidly from deep feelings of grief and flowing tears to laughter and joking with one another. Laughter had relieved tension on many occasions. After the laughter subsided, Roz continued:

I went back to Janet and did a lot of work for several months. One of the past lives that I went to was an Indian one; I was female and my son Running Deer, who was Michael, and I were adopted into your tribe after my people were killed. My name was Golden Hawk, and my husband's name was Man of the Rainbow, who I've been told I will meet. So, if any of you have seen him, tell him to come home.

Again we joined in spontaneous merriment at the idea of all of us looking for Roz's lost mate from another lifetime.

In June I located a studio and began to paint on canvas, an art form that I had not done for 18 years. I do abstract expressionism. I began to paint on six-foot by six-foot canvas—something very different from what I had intended to paint, but it seemed to be coming from inside me.

In August, DeLaine, Marda, Janet and I went for a vacation to visit Michael and Kate in Florida. Michael shared his regression with us, and as he talked I began to see the pictures. I had passed over a few months before the massacre and was in spirit, helping to pull the souls over to the other side. I remembered the confusion and turmoil of the souls and how I was trying to help all of you over. It wasn't until then that I realized, prompted by DeLaine, that what I had been painting for the past three months on the huge canvas was the image of the souls passing over after the massacre.

The paintings now just seem to come out of me. I don't always know what I'm painting until after it's done, and then I stand back and see it. When it's finished I'm going to have a show, and before opening night the members of the tribe will be invited for a private showing. For a few who have seen what I've done so far, I'm told it has been very healing. I have just finished a painting of Silver Eagle...

Roz took a deep breath and wiped his eyes.

...and it is quite devastating.

From Roz, sitting on the floor, the tissue box went to Robert, sitting on the couch with Kay, Vickie and Marilyn. Robert took time to think as he adjusted his glasses and slipped his hand into that of Kay, the woman with whom he now lived. Dot, his wife for 23 years, sat comfortably in a chair at the end of the couch. Their relationship had moved to one of honest friendship. He continued:

My memories of being in the tribe of Silver Eagle came in one of the earliest regressions of the group, September 3, 1986. I recently listened to the tape—there were separate regressions—and they brought up a lot of emotion again. I was Speckled Elk and I was an apprentice in training to the medicine man, who was Kay, my father. There was a baby born to me and another woman in the tribe; that baby was Elaine.

Elaine, seated across the room, smiled at Robert. He went on:

I had visions of the white men and what was to come. At the time of conflict in the tribe, a small group of us went away to a cave to die rather than fight.

He looked at Kay, recognizing her as his love now...and as his loving and wise father in that life. Kay had come into Robert's life about a year before, as he had begun dating again after he and Dot had officially separated. His relationship with Anna had also ended. My mind flashed to the years of counseling sessions and discussions that Robert and I had related to love and marriage. His world had been turned upside down when he met Anna, the woman who had been the baby's mother in that life.

How much healing has taken place within this group! I marveled, as Kay began to speak:

> *Well, I'm rather new to this. My only connection is the memory that Robert has and what others have told me, that I was a male, a medicine man of the tribe. I've had other regressions with Janet but not one to this Indian life. My name was White Cloud.*

Vickie spoke next. Her lightness and laughter defy the heaviness of excess weight on her body. She was 24 years old.

> *Kay was my mate in that life...I just realized that!*

From the time that they had met, Vickie and Kay had enjoyed a comfortable friendship. Vickie laughed at that idea.

> *I was 19 years old when I met Janet. Dot had gone to her to lose weight and she was excited about it and encouraged me. I remember thinking, She's not talking about hypnosis, is she? I met Janet, her sister-in-law Sara, whom some of you know, and became a part of the meditation circle, driving down every week from Ithaca.*
>
> *In the tribe I was very old at the time of the massacre; I seemed to have had something like Alzheimer's disease because I was very confused.*
>
> *I do want to say that sometimes now I see spirits around people. I'm seeing a lot of faces now over your faces. This room is really filled! I keep hearing the name "White Owl," and I don't know if it was someone's name or if it's someone's guide.*

"That's Timothy's name!" Marda exclaimed excitedly. Then, as if she had caught herself in her own accuracy, she put her hand over her mouth and whispered, "I think."

We all laughed as she explained, "I kept getting "White... White..., ' for Timothy, but I couldn't get the rest. When Vickie said, 'White Owl,' I knew that it was Timothy's name then."

The tissue box went to Marilyn, as she sighed in relief. "God, the tension in waiting around the circle until you got to this side!" Marilyn has a youthful appearance and looked especially attractive that evening. Her long strawberry blond hair fell over the white leather jacket that she wore over a black blouse and pants. As she felt her own emotion rise, she waited and looked tearfully to the ceiling.

If it weren't for some of the people in this room, I wouldn't even be here tonight.

Tears welled up in my eyes as I remembered the person whom I had met only two years earlier and the changes that Marilyn had made. She spoke softly and with much emotion.

My life centered around getting high and getting laid...and I had already tried suicide once and was considering it again. So, because of Janet, DeLaine, and Dot—the ones who were there first for me—I'm living a completely different life. I went through a lot of childhood and past-life regressions with Janet, and it was her idea for me to begin to put some of my emotion into my art work. Because of that and the belief that some of you showed in me, I recently had my first one-woman art show, which several of you came to. A lot of people came and over eighty percent of the pieces were sold. Now, I'm really living the life I've always dreamed of living, and I thank you all for it.

In the Indian lifetime I was known as Enar. I was an old woman, medicine woman to the tribe. Dot was my apprentice. I passed over before the massacre, and when I left I knew what was coming to the tribe.

Dot was sitting in a comfortable recliner. She was still a large woman, in spite of her 75-pound weight loss. Her short, curly dark brown hair neatly surrounded her face. I looked at my friend with whom I had worked intensely over a five-year period, and I smiled as Dot began to speak.

I'd like to lighten things up a bit by telling you about when I met Janet. I had known Janet socially and was quite aware of her reputation as a superwoman. She worked full time, had two sons, was active in community, church, and scouting activities, baked bread, and made her own granola.

One day I met her going to Scott's office. I saw her breeze into the office in her business suit, walk back and give her full attention to her husband and they left to go to lunch. I was certain that she and I would never have anything in common. In May, 1985, I went for an appointment with Janet to lose weight. We talked for over two hours and haven't stopped much since then.

In the tribe, as Marilyn said, I was preparing to become a medicine woman. My name in that life was Standing Tree, given to me by the medicine man.

I looked at Scott, my husband of 28 years. We were separated, physically living apart, but the love and support had not changed. He joked, "You've been waiting for this, haven't you?!"

I smiled. "I'm curious."

"I met this lady in 1955."

"Oh, you mean you're going back that far?"

"Basically, I'm a hillbilly from West Virginia, and she's..."

"Dynasty," Dot said, reminding Scott and me of the nicknames she gave us one day while shaking her head about our differences.

"So, how *did* you get together?" Michael joked.

"Fate...destiny," was my reply.

"Karma," came Marilyn's.

After the laughter had subsided I looked at Scott, knowing that aside from being my husband he very much had his own story in connection with this tribe and with his contribution to our coming together.

> *Maybe to bring Dan and Scottie into the world—most of you know these two great guys. It's interesting, when you look back on all those years, the decisions and choices that we made, the places that we lived, and the decisions that led us to come here. I've been told that I start things for others. One day I called a friend whom we call Mrs. D. and asked her to paint an Indian.*

"And this is what he started," whispered Scottie softly beside me.

As Scott stopped talking, the attention of the group moved to Elaine, looking like a pixie in her forties. Elaine is full of energy that she readily puts into an active business and family life. She smoothed her fashionable holiday outfit under her black velvet jacket.

> *I, too, knew Janet as superwoman, having met her at the church we attended. We had talked a few times because her son Scottie and my son were friends. One day, after one such conversation, she called and said, "My sister-in-law, Sara, will be visiting next week, and I wonder if you'd like to meet her."*
>
> *My first thought was, "Why would I want to do that?" I knew that Sara did psychic readings. After thinking about it, I decided to go to meet Sara, and when I did, she answered many things for me about my life.*
>
> *As Robert said, in the lifetime with Silver Eagle I was a baby. I did survive. A soldier took me home to live with him and his wife. But I felt so sad and out of place with the white people that I refused food and died.*
>
> *Janet invited me to the meditation circle and I went every week. For the first time in my life I felt that I had found a group of people where I belonged. I'm very grateful to the women in the Circle for all they've done to help me, and I pray that I don't do anything to bring disgrace to the tribe.*

Bring disgrace to the tribe? What in the world did she mean by that last sentence? That was so out of character for Elaine. We were certainly a group of individuals now, and it was not like Elaine even to think in such terms as disgrace, or shame. *What was that about?* My eyes caught Dot's immediately, but no words were spoken. The tissue box moved to Deb's hands.

> *This group has been through a lot with me, too. They've been there through some really tough times. My name in that life was Flaming Arrow. Today I sometimes refer to myself as Black Hawk Woman. I think I've had many, many Indian lives, and it disturbs me so much to see what we are doing to our land and the environment.... We should be ashamed, we should be ashamed!*

Her strong words changed to laughter.

> *I guess I'm really a radical son-of-a-bitch. Sometimes my daughter thinks so. I've just met Karen for the first time tonight, and I can't believe how much we have in common. We've joked about exchanging daughters for a while.*
> *In my regression I remembered the conflict in the tribe and how I wanted to stand and fight for the land.*

I had met Karen only two months earlier. Tonight she wore an authentic Sioux overshirt she had purchased some time ago. Everything she wore seemed to emphasize her wide, intense blue eyes. As Deb handed her the tissue box, I wondered what she thought of all of this, it was so new to her.

> *I met Roz through my shop. I have a lot of Native American art. In fact, I bought a weaving by Roz before I even met him. One day he walked into my shop and showed me some photographs of his work; I pointed to it and said, "I have that weaving!" He smiled, held out his hand, and said, "Shake hands with the artist."*
> *I had been going through some rather difficult times and Roz told me about Janet. He mentioned some past-life regressions that he had done. Now, I consider myself very open*

minded, and I thought, Well, that's okay for you, but it's not for me. One day he invited me to see his paintings, and I was so taken by them I just couldn't get them out of my mind. His creativity was impressive, and he said, "If it weren't for Janet I wouldn't be doing this." I called her the next day.

My regression went to what we think was a different Indian life, and I thought I was making it up except for the emotion that came—I couldn't explain that away. Also, I kept feeling an actual burning sensation in my nose that wouldn't leave and a dryness and parched throat.

When Sara recently came up for a weekend visit I went to coffee with her and Janet. She sat down across from me in a booth and whispered, "Janet, she was in the massacre!" We had to ask the waitress for extra napkins. She said my name was Little Blue Mountain and that I was tortured by fire.

My logical mind kept fighting the idea, but it makes so much sense to who I am and everything that I've felt since I was a child that I can't explain it away. Learning this and seeing Roz's paintings have been very healing for me.

Karen handed the box to me. I took a deep breath.

I was female, about 14 years old at the time of the massacre. The Grandfathers said that I was to be the next chief—we didn't know that it would be many lifetimes later—and that as chief my purpose would be to gather the tribe together again and help heal the wounds from such horrendous memories.

I've been encouraged to write the story, and I've started to take steps to do that. I know that in writing it I have to allow my own memories and (I looked up at the faces around my living room with tears in my eyes, as I caught my breath), as you know, I have preferred and trusted your memories more than my own. Now, in the writing, I have to face my own experience of that lifetime and what it was to me.

I have no idea what direction the story will go. Perhaps it will simply be a few photocopies that we pass around and share—or perhaps Linda Evans will play me in the movie.

My unexpected move to humor in the midst of tears surprised everyone. In the laughter, Michael and Scottie said simultaneously, "Shirley MacLaine would be more appropriate." I went on:

> *It will be written as my story, with some identities fictionalized to protect the privacy of anyone who wants that. I'll let you each decide if you prefer to use your own name or a fictitious one. I hope to use portions of Roz's paintings and some of Michael's poetry (my seminar-leader self took over), which we'll hear read by Kate after we stand, stretch, and take a break.*

As we gathered together again, I asked Scottie to share what he had mentioned to me during our break.

> *When the painting arrived at our house and I looked at it, I remember my reaction was anger, and my thoughts were, "What nerve you have! Don't you dare come here after what you did." All the time I've been sitting here listening to you all talk, I've been feeling anger rising, there is tightness in my jaw and now I have a headache. I guess Mom and I are going to be doing a regression while I'm home.*

Kate's soft and lilting voice filled the room as she began, saying, "In addition to our celebration together, today is also Janet's birthday, so we thought in honor of that, the first poem I'll read is about Janet." As she read a poem Michael had mailed to me three months earlier I could not stop the tears that ran down over my face.

Chapter XI

An Explosion of Memories:
Late December 1990 through January 1991

The next morning Michael called me to say, "Okay, you asked me a question and I woke with the answer. See how this sounds to you. Scottie's name was Walks Among Horses. He had a special place of honor in the tribe in his connection with the horses."

As with each new piece of information about the tribe, I filed this name away for later confirmation. Scottie planned to undergo a regression the following day, but first I had to meet with Marda's nephew Timothy for a session.

Timothy

I had a light breakfast and dressed. I didn't think Timothy would mind if I dressed casually wearing jeans and a red wool sweater instead of business attire, which I usually wear at my office, where I would be meeting him for his first regression. He had asked me last night, "How do you feel when you are going to do one of these regressions, Janet?"

My usual "Fine" came out too quickly. The truth was that whenever I did a past-life regression I really did not know where the person would go. I had found, however, that the more I connected with my own emotions, the stronger my personal reactions became to these tribal memories. And my reactions had begun to grow more intense.

Even though Timothy had attended the Celebration Party on the previous night, his presence there was no indication that his unconscious mind would automatically move to that incarnation—*unless* such a move was a priority for him. Often if, based on personal thoughts or a psychic reading, a client expects to see a particular lifetime, that person is surprised to find that this does not occur. Therefore, it was possible that Timothy's mind could take him to a different experience that was affecting him.

As I drove to the office I pictured Marda being present in the room during this regression, and I wondered if it would work out that way. It did—Timothy asked if Marda could be present, and it turned out that she was available and willing to do so. I felt pleased, knowing that Marda's energy would not interfere with Timothy and that her presence would be beneficial for their continued discussions afterward. There was a relationship between nephew and aunt that had always been close and positive. Marda had already told Timothy not to be disappointed if he did not see the Indian lifetime in case that did not take place.

As I began the induction I watched Timothy's mind struggle. I knew that he was trying to perceive clearly, in spite of his experience of the night before. He didn't want his regression to be colored by what he had heard others say. Timothy kept repeating, "I don't know," as if to stop his own memory from coming.

Janet: *Where are you and what is happening?*
Timothy: *I just see shadows. There's a fire. I just feel sad. I don't know, I see shadows...I feel sad, but I don't know why. I seem to be moving around.*
Janet: *Where are you in conjunction with the fire?*
Timothy: *It's in between the shadows.*

I directed him to move his energy more into his body in that time and space.

Timothy: *Moving...I'm dancing...it's night. I'm...don't see any-thing....*

Janet: *Tell me about what you're feeling as you dance.*
Timothy: *I'm getting carried away in the passion—carried away.*

I watched Timothy's body as he sat in the chair under a blanket for warmth. Both feet, on the recliner extension, moved rhythmically in a perfect beat. I pointed this out to Marda, who noted it with a smile.

Janet: *Why are you dancing?*
Timothy: *I don't know...I don't know anything. I'm trying to let go, I can't let go. All I feel is fighting within me to let go, and I can't. I'm just thinking that...I can't do it. I want to let it go, but I don't want to feel it again. My face is tingling, it's dry, my face is tingling. It's very dark, everything is very black. It's nighttime.*
Janet: *Are there others around, or are you alone?*
Timothy: *There are others dancing. All I see is a straight line; there could be a circle, but on this side it's a straight line. I just feel like it's a circle around the fire, many around the fire—friends, family—they're my people.*

Emotion suddenly began to build and Timothy's entire energy changed. From being a pleasant and quiet-natured young man, he grew powerful, strong, and all masculine.

Timothy: *Everyone knows what's happening. It's all happening too fast!*
Janet: *What's happening?*

With deep emotion Timothy cried out.

Timothy: *I don't know!*

Timothy's strong masculine energy now filled the room as his chin moved up and his chest burst out. His voice became deeper and with force he spoke loudly.

Timothy: *I've got to stop them...we've got to stop them from coming! This is our right! Stay away! This is our right! We have*

> *Great Spirit on our side. This is our right! Stay away! Stay*
> *away! Oh...*

Janet: *Who is it? Who is coming?*

Timothy: *I don't know. They don't belong!*

His torment changed and he became calm.

Janet: *What is it?*

Timothy: *I'm going with what feels right. I'm moving and I know it*
feels right. It's all I have...all I have is the dance.

Janet: *What is happening now?*

Timothy: *It feels as if there is a decision, a conclusion. All we have*
is each other, and each other's strength.

Janet: *And tell me about this decision.*

Timothy: *My hands are warm, my face is cold. I stop moving. My*
friends are with me and we stand as one, for what's right.
I'm not afraid. I don't feel...I don't see anything but
shadows by the fire.

I directed Timothy to stay within that lifetime and move to the
next significant event. What he did next only mildly surprised me.

Timothy: *It's soft and peaceful...feel the air around me...it's okay.*
I'm very cold, it's very cold.... I don't see anyone or any-
thing.... I feel like a conclusion...getting away from it.
Nothing to do but let go. I think I've died. I feel like I was
above it. Maybe I was Michael's guide. Maybe I wasn't
there....

Timothy's unconscious mind appeared to be fighting between re-
living the experience and wanting to avoid this memory entirely. I
decided to remain silent and give him some time. He was the one
who spoke next.

Timothy: *I can't get away and I'm stuck in this purgatory and this*
limbo of in-between and I can't go there and I can't get
away from there and I'm stuck.

I guided Timothy again to feel his energy in the body at that time and space. He suddenly found himself back in the experience.

Timothy: We have to fight...we have to fight. We can't let them do this to us. They have no right!

The masculine-warrior-energy exploded out in anguish as he yelled.

Timothy: How can you sit there...you are our leader! How can you say, "Leave it be and accept his ways!" (With a furious anger.) We have no choice! No choice but to stand as one, and maybe to die as one. But then we'll be with Great Spirit...we won't have to succumb to any of this. If none of you will fight, then I will—and I will fight alone!

Tears rolled down my face as I tried to stay grounded to guide the regression while also being *in* it. I looked at Marda's bowed head as she sat in a chair next to Timothy and was herself pulled into the memory. I saw the furious warrior, White Owl, as he shouted at the chief.

Timothy: I'll have Great Spirit on my side. You sit there...and your prophesies say that Great Spirit will come. What do you know! You know nothing! I know! And I'll not let it happen...I cannot let it happen!

With excruciating torment, White Owl yelled.

*Timothy: **You're our chief! Do something! Do something! Don't just sit there! Do something! How can you be our chief and not be of strength? We're falling apart. We have no strength!***

Wiping my eyes with tissues, and composing myself, I tried to make my voice sound as in-control and professional as possible.

Janet: What do you do?
Timothy: Music...some of us have united and we dance as one, and Great Spirit goes with us. We dance. I feel so alone in this

> *group of one. I feel so cold...and I feel so angry. I want to touch someone, I want to hold someone...but I can't... because I have to be strong. I have no wisdom, but I have strength...and my strength is my wisdom. I've come to no resolution within this resolution. I'm so angry and so uneasy. The flesh moves and we are one with the earth...I can feel the animals...the animal spirits within us all.*

I directed Timothy to move to the next significant event that was affecting him.

Timothy: *Horses...riding...there is confusion all around. There's a strength around...fighting with the strength of spirit all around me...nothing can harm me. I am strong...I fly with spirit.*

A sudden jerk of his body.

Janet: *What is it?*
Timothy: *My head hurts.*
Janet: *What has happened?*
Timothy: *I don't know, it really hurts. It's okay now...I have to go...okay...it will be okay.*

I recognize that he had gone into spirit.

Timothy: *I just see black, there's nothing but black...there's one Light, near...I can't...a peaceful blackness. I want to go back. Why do I have the arrow in me? I don't know...I don't know...I just see an arrow.*
Janet: *Where is the arrow?*
Timothy: *Right in my chest...in the middle. I saw that before, but I didn't think...but why? Why is it there? I see me lying there...and I want to go back. I tried to, but I can't. I really don't want to let it go. Why is there an arrow in me?*

I asked if he could see or remember what happened to him.

Timothy: *I fell off the horse and...I don't know. Everyone was everywhere...people everywhere. I don't know...I can't see anything. I just see confusion...confusion, I can't see anything. They're very close, very close...everyone is everywhere...a great...I just, just...closed-in feeling...of all these people together...it's because...our people...I don't want to kill anymore. I don't want to kill. I don't want to fight. Where are my...where are my friends?*

Janet: *Where are you now?*

Timothy: *I don't know...I just want a friend there—there's no one. I don't know, I'm alone. I just...just let me go, let me go. There's no pain. I don't feel any pain. I don't know.*

I asked Timothy to be aware of his thoughts as his spirit left his physical body. He spoke with a soft voice and deep emotion.

Timothy: *I'm so sorry! I am so sorry that we fought. I was so wrong. I was just so wrong. I chose strength over wisdom. There is no wisdom in strength. Wisdom is the strength. I just feel very responsible. I feel that...have this guilt and I have to leave...leave. It was my fault. I yelled and I argued and I was so young. I knew nothing. I didn't know anything...but I thought I did. I thought I knew everything. I...I have...let go, and go on.*

I directed him to move to the Light and feel the love and acceptance.

Timothy: *It's okay...I'm home. It's all...so far away now...it's far away....*

Again I gave suggestions to let go of the guilt and feel the Light and Love.

Timothy: *I knew we would all be together again.... I didn't know it would be so soon after.... We're all together and it's okay...where we are. There's nothing but the love we shared and it's okay. We're here and we share this love. We're here.*

After I slowly brought Timothy back into the room, encouraging him to feel the release from his heart and mind, the three of us took a few moments for deep breaths, for wiping our eyes and shifting positions.

"But I don't understand...the arrow in me...," Timothy continued to wonder. Marda started to speak and stopped herself.

"Go on," I encouraged her.

"I didn't want to say it...but I saw you put the arrow into your own chest."

This made sense...and it felt right. Timothy's mind would have had difficulty and fought that memory. White Owl could stand it no longer. As with many in the tribe, he had so much self-blame—he wanted out. The arrow had been his own.

A few weeks later, while I discussed Timothy's regression with Roz, he reminded me of a dream that he had had months earlier. He had told me about it at the time. In the dream Roz saw an Indian warrior and watched as this warrior plunged an arrow into his own chest. At the time we didn't know what this dream could be about. Now we knew. Roz's spirit had rushed to White Owl to guide him to the other side.

Kate

Timothy was not the only one to need release of buried emotions. Before coming to New York for the Celebration, Kate told me that she felt she needed another regression. She recognized that something was rising within her...and she felt fear. Kate, as is true with most of the people in this tribe, decided that this feeling of fear was an indication of something that she needed to bring from her unconscious mind to release.

We scheduled her appointment for the afternoon after the party. Following Timothy's session I went home, fixed lunch, and took a nap to be sure I would be refreshed and alert for Kate's appointment. I honestly did not expect that Kate would go to that same Indian lifetime. I expected her to reach another past life, but I was wrong.

As usual, I asked Kate's unconscious mind to "move to an event or memory that is affecting you now." Suddenly she started to breathe quickly. I felt fear from her...short quick breaths.

> Kate: *I'm running...my heart is pounding.*
> Janet: *Okay, feel yourself running...stay in the running...feel your heart pounding. Why are you running? What is happening?*
> Kate: *Someone is chasing me...(Continued short breaths...) I'm hiding, I'm under a bush.*

After a while I asked Kate to move ahead in time, but she could not move from that position. I recognized her fear of the next experience. So I encouraged her to stay under the bush a while longer and, sensing the right time, tried again.

> Kate: *My hands are going numb, prickly.*

Kate began rubbing her hands and shaking them as if to feel any feeling in them.

> Kate: *My hands are tied. I see a man in black boots, blue pants, and shirt.... (Again shaking her hands.) I can't feel my hands...a torch...a man has a torch. He's lighting the hem of my dress!*

I knew that Kate needed to experience this memory so she could release it. On my knees beside the chair, I set my hand on her shoulder as assurance of my presence, and I continued to guide her through the memories.

> Kate: *My legs are numb...I smell the smoke, feel the dryness in my mouth and nostrils...blackness....*

This regression had actually completed the puzzle for Kate. During her previous regression her unconscious mind had been unable to release the memory of torture, so she believed that she had lived. Now she knew what had happened to her at the end of that life.

The memories of this entire group of people were amazing—and as these memories surfaced we continued to heal ourselves of our pain, grief, self-blame, fear, anger, and hatred. Sometimes only bits of information or emotion would arise—only what we could deal with at the time.

Scottie

On the next afternoon Scottie came for his session. Timothy's and Kate's regressions had proven to be so powerful that I questioned the wisdom of regressing my own son. *No one can do it better than you,* I said to myself as Scottie and I drove to my office.

Once we arrived, Scottie settled comfortably into what we referred to as the "hypnosis chair." When he had been younger he had remarked, "Mom, this chair has sleepy vibrations in it." He found that still to be true and quickly drifted into a deep state.

Scottie is a young man of few words, and he remained so deeply under hypnosis that he needed considerable prodding to get the words out. Unlike Timothy, who had "re-lived" his experience with much emotion, Scottie remained cool and calm as he methodically described what he saw.

Janet:	*Tell me what you are seeing, feeling, or perceiving.*
Scottie:	*A stream, with sun shining down on the water.*
Janet:	*Good, and where are you?*
Scottie:	*I'm close to the stream.*
Janet:	*Now, moving into this experience more and more deeply, more and more completely. I want you to feel your own body in that time and space. Look down at your feet and tell me what you are wearing on your feet, if anything.*
Scottie:	*Moccasins.*
Janet:	*Okay, and moving on up your body, can you tell me what more you are wearing?*
Scottie:	*Loin...just a loincloth.*
Janet:	*Okay, and moving on up your body, can you tell me if you are wearing anything on your chest? Tell me about your*

	face, your hair, or if you are wearing anything on your head.
Scottie:	*Necklace...it's a leather string, with something in the middle, like a stone or pendant-type thing. Just a band around the head.*
Janet:	*Are you male or female?*
Scottie:	*Male.*
Janet:	*Approximately how old are you?*
Scottie:	*Twenty-three...?*

I watched Scottie's conscious mind enter, questioning his age.

Janet:	*What is the color of your skin?*
Scottie:	*Kind of dark.*
Janet:	*Now, being at the stream, tell me what you are doing or what brings you here.*
Scottie:	*There are horses behind me.*
Janet:	*What are you doing?*
Scottie:	*Sitting at the stream.*
Janet:	*Is anyone else with you, or are you alone?*
Scottie:	*Alone.*
Janet:	*Okay, I want you to tune into your mind in that time and space and tell me how you are feeling.*
Scottie:	*Calm, relaxed. I'm carving on something, whittling something.*
Janet:	*How many horses do you have with you?*
Scottie:	*The whole tribe's.*
Janet:	*How does this happen? What are you doing with them?*
Scottie:	*Just watching them, taking them to water, to drink occasionally.*
Janet:	*Now, in just a few moments, I'm going to have you move back to where your tribe is, but before I do, is there anything else that you are sensing or perceiving in that space that should be mentioned?*
Scottie:	*I'm feeling a nervousness now.*
Janet:	*And why is that?*
Scottie:	*Just wondering of the things to come, I believe.*
Janet:	*Okay, let's move back to where the tribe is...on the count of three, move back to where your people are. Number one—staying within this lifetime and going back to where*

	your people are. Number two—moving. Number three—tell me what you are doing and what is happening.
Scottie:	*Just walking through the village toward a tepee.*
Janet:	*Is this the tepee where you reside, where you live, or someone else's?*
Scottie:	*It's someone else's.*
Janet:	*Okay, see yourself going to this tepee, and tell me what is happening.*
Scottie:	*I'm going inside, and there is a circle of people, all men.*
Janet:	*What is this circle for? What is happening?*
Scottie:	*It's a meeting.*
Janet:	*Can you tell me about these men in the circle?*
Scottie:	*Umm…just discussing amongst ourselves…the meeting hasn't started yet.*
Janet:	*What is the atmosphere?*
Scottie:	*Tension. It's…I still get a feeling of people sharpening things.*
Janet:	*Okay, allow time to pass, and as the meeting begins, tell me what is happening.*
Scottie:	*Someone else comes into the tent.*
Janet:	*Tell me about this person.*
Scottie:	*Big, strong…has, like pants and shirt on, an Indian; I believe it's the chief. Comes in, sits down. Then we all listen to him.*
Janet:	*What is it that he is saying? What is this meeting about?*
Scottie:	*People arguing, shaking their fists.*
Janet:	*What are they arguing about?*
Scottie:	*Moving, moving the tribe. And some people want to stay and some want to leave.*
Janet:	*Can you tell me what you want to do? How are you feeling? What do you want to do?*
Scottie:	*I don't know.*
Janet:	*Okay, can you tell me what the chief is advising?*
Scottie:	*(Deep breath.) I believe he is asking who will stay.*
Janet:	*Okay, and as you look around the circle of men, can you tell me more about the attitude of the men there? Who will stay and who will go? What is the attitude of the group?*
Scottie:	*They want to stay.*
Janet:	*Can you tell me anything more about what is going on before we move ahead in time?*

Scottie:	*Just arguing.*
Janet:	*Once again on the count of three I want you to move ahead in time, staying within this lifetime and moving ahead to the next significant event that is affecting you now. One—moving ahead, it might be a matter of minutes, hours, days, or weeks. Two—staying within this lifetime. Three—allow the perceptions to come in.*
Scottie:	*A lot of soldiers.*
Janet:	*What is happening?*
Scottie:	*They've come into the village, and we're not ready for it.*
Janet:	*Where are you?*
Scottie:	*Center of the...I've come out of the tepee and running, grabbing weapons....*
Janet:	*Tell me more about what is happening. What are the soldiers doing?*
Scottie:	*They're shooting and killing everybody.*
Janet:	*And what of the people? What are they doing? How are they fighting?*
Scottie:	*They're running, trying to run, hide, protect each other. Women are running and grabbing the children.*
Janet:	*Continue to see what is happening, and tell me what you see.*

Scottie spoke in a calm, emotionless voice as he described the scene.

Scottie:	*Men are on horses...the soldiers are on horses. Our horses are by the stream...trampling, trampling over people ...and...everything.*
Janet:	*Where are you, what are you doing now?*
Scottie:	*I'm fighting with a hatchet in my right hand and a knife in my left hand.*
Janet:	*Who is around you? Is anyone helping?*
Scottie:	*No. Killed one soldier, hit him in the stomach with my hatchet, pull him off his horse and cut his throat as he was falling to the ground. Just leave him there, moving on to the next soldier.*
Janet:	*How are you feeling?*
Scottie:	*Angry. The next soldier rides closer. He's on my left, fires a shot and misses, and as he continues to ride by, I bury*

	my hatchet into his back, turn around...and all I have left is my knife.
Janet:	*What do you do now?*
Scottie:	*Just standing, waiting for more to come at me. Now running to help another Indian. He's fighting with a soldier on a horse. I jump up onto the horse...bury my knife into his chest...and throw him off the horse...and then a soldier riding by on another horse jumps on me and takes me off the horse and I land on my friend's knife, into my back. I'm still trying to fight the soldier, but he's too strong...and my friend helps me, and kills the soldier, pulls him off me.*
Janet:	*Allow the first thought that flows through your mind. Can you tell me the name of your friend?*
Scottie:	*Starts with S—Sitting....*
Janet:	*Okay, allow it to be for right now..."Sitting." If the name is important, it will come to you.[4] Continue now to see what is happening? What are you doing?*
Scottie:	*I'm rolling onto my right side, trying to get up...I'm running to fight...(Long pause.)...trying to take another soldier off a horse. He strikes me in the back of the head...I fall to the ground...and...I must have died...I'm kind of looking down on the village from up top now.*
Janet:	*Okay, feel your spirit being free of the body, feel yourself looking down on the village and tell me what you're seeing.*
Scottie:	*Just soldiers riding through the village, cutting people, cutting people with their swords...I see Indians running toward the stream...soldiers, a couple of soldiers try to get them, but most of them are busy tearing apart the village.*
Janet:	*What is happening now?*
Scottie:	*It's over.*

The Paintings

The next day Scottie and I joined Michael and Kate and visited Roz's studio to see his paintings. As always, I found it fascinating to hear their comments as they studied the enormous panels of souls passing into spirit.

Michael said, "I see a fetus." I had thought that he knew White Fawn (DeLaine) had been pregnant at the time of her death, but he had not known this before seeing the fetus in Roz's work.

As we stared at the painting of Silver Eagle I felt the slightest urgings of memory from my unconscious. Suddenly I saw the flash of a picture—Little Feather's (Marda's) death. I leaned toward Michael and whispered, "I just saw Little Feather with a rifle in her mouth."

"Was she alone?" Michael asked, "Lying on the ground?" He had seen the same image.

We stayed in the studio with Roz's paintings for a long time, finding much to see in them. Roz shared with us his experiences of painting the face of the chief. At several points he had found himself backing up against the wall, overcome with emotion, before he could continue.

Roz had asked Michael to pose for some photographs to assist him in the paintings yet to come, as Michael's body was perfect to portray the Indian of that time. Karen had loaned some Native American pieces from her gallery for Michael to wear. Kate told me later that there were times when the pictures that Roz could see through the camera lens and the picture that he saw from his memory-vision became intertwined. Michael's body looked like that of Running Deer in that earlier life, and Running Deer looked just like Roz's mate, the one who had died.

Roz climbed a ladder to get shots looking down, having arranged Michael's body on the floor. Kate said that Roz suddenly let out a gasp...climbed down from the ladder and backed away, looking as if he had seen a ghost.

It amazed me how each of us continued to help release one another's unconscious memories. And we did this with the most loving support and intentions. For instance, Roz had a channeling session with Dot who had sensed his name in that life: Golden Hawk. When I gave small Christmas gifts to Kate and Michael and Roz, I glanced at the name that I had written on the envelope, "Golden Winged Hawk," as I handed it to him. He read it and looked up at me with a glow on his face.

"Golden Winged Hawk! That's my name." I hadn't even realized that I had written it differently from what he had told me. Michael

Running Deer

would be another who would know, and he nodded with a sense of memory.

"The name Golden Hawk didn't feel complete," Roz said, "but now it is complete. That's my name. Thank you."

Memories through Bodywork

Our healing work continued, not only through Roz's artwork and our individual regressions but also through DeLaine's bodywork. On DeLaine's massage table Kate suddenly remembered that in the Indian lifetime her mother had died in childbirth. The baby who had been born, her little sister, was Marda—Little Feather. This explained for Kate a very subtle coolness that she had always felt toward Marda and had not understood. As a child Kate, known as Little Star, had blamed the baby for her mother's death. Marda had felt Kate's mysterious coolness and now was pleased that the two had learned its source so they could resolve the vague uneasiness that had existed between them.

During Kate's bodywork session with DeLaine, Roz had waited for her in the next room. There he stretched out on a couch and drifted in and out of sleep. But as he dozed off he sensed the spirit presence of a young girl in the room and told the women about it. Later, once they were alone, Kate told Roz, "I think that you sensed DeLaine's daughter Lynette, who passed away." Kate felt that Lynette had come back to assist in DeLaine's healing, as well as her own, as some things had remained unresolved between them.

Roz paused for a moment. "I feel that I'd like to paint White Fawn (DeLaine) in that life," he told Kate. "She was my friend and she helped the tribe so much. I feel that DeLaine needs a lot of healing. Maybe I can include Lynette in the painting, to further the healing between them."

DeLaine had hoped to join the rest of us from the "Florida Group" when we gathered at Marda's house that week for a holiday luncheon. But sometimes the push that we give each other—just with our presence—can become too intense. DeLaine came down with the flu and could not join us. She questioned why she had brought this illness to herself right at that time.

Roz, Michael, and Kate met me at Marda's home. They loved her A-frame house and enjoyed gazing out the large glass windows that faced the woods. She had built a fire in the wood stove that warmed the dining area, where she had already set a table.

Michael put his arm around Marda; her small body fit neatly under his arm. I told her that I had seen a mental picture of the end of her life as the Indian child Little Feather, and that a rifle had been in her mouth. Michael continued, "She wasn't killed by the rifle, but there was lots of metal in her body."

"Oh, oh," she cried as the truth of those swords and knives came to her, "and I thought that I had no memories of that lifetime." Marda had buried those memories deep in her unconscious. They would remain buried until she felt strong enough to handle them. Her body, however, "remembered" and continued to respond to metal, including the braces on her teeth. I had never met anyone so allergic to metal.

Marda

Meanwhile, Michael cleared his throat and pretended to be preparing for a major address. With a few kind words he presented me with a very special gift—a round-trip ticket to Naples, Florida, from this special trio—Kate and Roz and himself. "We're serious about your writing this book," Roz said.

After our luncheon gathering ended, Marda kept an appointment to see an iridologist that evening. Marda had been dealing with a great deal of stress during the holiday season. The iridologist looked into her eyes and offered information related to Marda's health and family issues—for example, that Marda's mother was a diabetic.

"My, these braces are giving you a terrible time," she added and proceeded to tell Marda that they had been applied without first adjusting her jaw. She also said, "You had a fall when you were a child and were knocked unconscious for awhile." Marda had no such recollection but the woman said, "Just think about it, you'll remember." They ended their session with instructions for a very strict regime of herbs and a rigid diet for cleansing.

Six inches of snow fell that night, so Marda had to stay overnight with a friend. Feeling stressed out and tense, she awakened the next morning to drive home, change clothes, and get to work. While scraping the ice off her windshield she broke a fingernail and released a startling emotional outburst with a yell into the air, "What do you have to do, break me?" She cried hysterically—and at that point saw a flashback to her childhood (in this life)—of being sexually molested by her brother. She had fallen and was knocked unconscious.

When she arrived home Marda called me to ask, "Is it possible, Janet, that you can block out something from *this lifetime* so totally? Am I making it up?" I assured her that the mind has the capacity to blank out something completely, and in the light of the tears that streamed down both our faces throughout the telephone conversation, neither of us believed that she had made it up. *What an incredible time of healing the end of 1990 brings to her,* I thought. *She has learned how she died in the Indian lifetime, has gained health information, and retrieved an unthinkable memory.* Her brother had committed suicide just a few years earlier.

I was glad to learn that Marda and her husband were going away for a vacation over the New Year holiday. She certainly needed and deserved the rest.

That Christmas both Scott and Scottie joined me for Christmas dinner. Our older son, Dan, was in Germany, visiting his cousin Ginger and her husband. It was interesting to me that during this time of "tribal reunion" Dan and Ginger, two other members of our tribe, were together in Germany.

I had not yet looked deeply at my own memories of the tribe. As soon as we could arrange some time during this holiday visit, Michael and I tried a regression for me. He sat down on the floor nearby after turning my telephone ringer off. I made myself comfortable on the futon-couch, sitting cross-legged, with a blanket wrapped around my shoulders. I put myself into an altered state of consciousness and immediately saw a handsome Indian walking among tepees. The Indian looked up and saw a falling star. At that point I knew that my name in that life was what I had always recognized to be my soul name, Falling Star.

I leaned forward in a light trance state as I described to Michael the peaceful village and loving cooperation among our people and then the confusion and fear that arose. I began to sense what I called the "white faces." Then I suddenly stopped talking and sat back on the couch.

"What just happened?" Michael asked.

"Everything stopped," I replied. My mind had suddenly cut off the memory and I could perceive nothing outside of sitting on the couch talking with Michael. Seven more weeks would pass before I would feel strong enough for my unconscious mind to release those memories.

Meanwhile, when the holidays ended and Marda had returned from her vacation, she met DeLaine and me for lunch. The three of us sat at a small square table in a restaurant overlooking the Susquehanna River on Riverow in Owego. Marda told DeLaine about her recent spontaneous memories of having been sexually molested by her brother at age seven.

That evening DeLaine phoned and said, "Janet while I was working on a client (in an altered state), I kept getting pictures of Marda in the Indian life. See if this makes sense to you." *I knew immediately what DeLaine was going to say.* She went on, "Marda's brother was a soldier in that life—he was the one who raped and killed her." I confirmed to DeLaine that I thought she was right and told her yes when she asked, "Do you think I should tell her? I also sense that in this life her father knew what had happened with her brother."

I felt as if I had reached the end of my shock-level. I thought back to what I knew of Marda's childhood, to her father's alcoholism, and to how she had stored all the pain. She had stored it so deeply that she indicated no childhood problems before a few years ago, and she would not—could not—remember the lifetime as Little Feather. Had her brother been one of the soldiers? All of my senses said yes.

I thought of the few people who I knew had been soldiers in that lifetime. Several had created a hell for themselves in their current life. *Is that how it works?* I wondered. *The punishment is no longer* *necessary. Let's stop the persecution, the self-blame, the self-punishment. Soldiers, Indians, blacks, women, homosexuals, Christians, Jews—**stop creating hell and start creating heaven!***

Chapter XII

Healing of the Tribe: Early January 1991

DeLaine

DeLaine phoned to ask, "What are you doing Tuesday? I've got some free time, and thought we could get together for..."

"A regression?" *...the words flew out of my mouth!* I seldom suggest that a person have a regression—I wait for them to make that decision, usually when their discomfort reaches a peak.

I felt DeLaine's intake of breath as she stumbled, "...Uh...a regression? ...I thought, maybe we could have lunch."

A few days later we talked, and DeLaine admitted, "When you said regression, I felt fear go through my whole body!"

"I know," I said. "I felt it."

"Maybe I do need to have one," she said, hesitating. "Are you free on Wednesday morning?"

As I checked my calendar I knew that she would be relieved if I were busy, but my calendar does not seem to "work that way"—I was free to do the regression that I knew she needed.

On Wednesday morning DeLaine walked down the stairs to my office, dressed comfortably in jeans and a bright green sweater. She had heard an internal message to avoid eating before she came to see me. We both knew that food can serve to stuff down emotions, and I felt happy to see that she was willing to listen to what she had heard. She was also aware of a great deal of pain in her right shoulder.

She handed me a letter that Kate had written to her, a straightforward and loving letter that said that DeLaine's issue was not DeLaine and husband, but DeLaine and DeLaine. Kate had gone on to refer to DeLaine's strong control, and that eventually we all have to give up control if we expect to move on. Kate also referred to the energy that Roz had sensed when he had been in the house—energy of DeLaine's deceased daughter, Lynette. Kate said she felt that Lynette had returned for the healing that needed to occur between her and her mother.

This would not be DeLaine's first regression. In addition to the group regression several years earlier, DeLaine had tried to move into another life, but we agreed that she had "controlled" it, not allowing the full memory to emerge from her unconscious mind. She had experienced a meaningful regression to the tribe and remembered herself as White Fawn. "Silver Eagle called me that," she had said, "because I was swift and gentle and loving. He made me feel so special. He made all of us feel special. He said my eyes were like those of a doe." She had remembered that Margaret Osborne, as Silver Eagle's other mate, had been unable to bear children and that White Fawn "bore strong healthy babies."

During her earlier regression DeLaine had felt powerful body sensations—as if something, or someone, were being ripped from her body—but she had remained unable to see what was happening. We knew that as White Fawn in her Indian life she had been pregnant at the time of her death. She believed the unborn infant to be the same soul as Lynette.

At that time DeLaine had seen that she had refused to look at Silver Eagle in the end, crying, "I can't look at him, I can't look at him." Only then did she realize the anger that she had felt toward him.

DeLaine believed, also, that her present husband in this life had been a soldier in that earlier incarnation. "He wasn't one of the military men in command," she said. "He was young—he had the job of cleaning up the mess after it was all over."

I lit the orchid candle and a small soft light and switched off the overhead lamp. I asked DeLaine to begin to put herself into an altered state and told her I would step in and guide. I turned on a piece of higher consciousness music and, as always, said a mental prayer asking for guidance. I began to connect her with her Higher Self and with White Light energy. She moved quickly into an altered state. As I continued a limited induction, I rose from my chair and moved closer, asking, "What is happening?"

A gasp came out of her mouth, which she covered quickly with her hand. "Silver Eagle wants to take me back...to hold the infant." I encouraged that movement, and soon she found herself deep in the experience—no controlling this time! I set a cushion on the floor and kneeled down beside her as she began to sob.

> She's so beautiful...skin so soft. Oh, she's so beautiful, black eyes.... I wondered where she got those black eyes. She didn't have a chance...they killed her.... How could they have killed her...? So innocent...I couldn't help her...I couldn't save them...I couldn't help any of them...I tried.... Oh, I'm holding her.

I handed DeLaine tissues as her sobbing increased. She was seeing the unborn infant in the past life and Lynette in this life. "Let it come," I encouraged her. "Let the tears come—they've been held in much too long."

She cried for a long time—tears for a baby of that Indian lifetime, a baby who had never been born, and tears for her first-born child in this life, a child who had chosen death at age 19. I placed my hand on her shoulder and handed her more tissues, taking some for myself.

> He (DeLaine's husband) tried to make it up to her (Lynette)...but he couldn't. She kept running away. He tried to give love to her, but he didn't know how.... I didn't understand...I wanted him to give me attention, but he gave all his attention to her.... I didn't understand...he hates himself, oh how he hates himself...there is so much anger...anger at himself.

The fight was between him and her—I thought it was me.... It wasn't me...he tried to make it up to her.

I remembered the time of Lynette's sudden death, remembered the shock that we had felt over this beautiful young woman who had taken her own life. I remembered DeLaine's unbelievable control at the funeral home, consoling everyone else. I thought of how DeLaine's husband visits Lynette's grave so often, and I watched as the tears that had not been shed fourteen years ago now poured forth.

One of the reasons DeLaine had kept her power down, had given in to her husband so much since our return from Florida, had to do with his health—he might die. Her daughter had died without a sense of peace between them. This same thing might also happen with him.

I can't help him...I've tried.... I can't explain to him.... He wouldn't understand.... I can't do anything.

"No—you cannot," I said. "Now, you let go and trust his own soul to guide him in the path that is right for him—to stay or to leave, to get well or to become ill—let go, and allow."

Her mind moved between current reality with her husband and her now-deceased daughter and her lifetime as White Fawn, mate of Silver Eagle.

My friend...she came to our tribe...I helped her...but she didn't want to stay...she left...she missed him so much.

I listened—who was she talking about? Her next words told me:

She kept looking for her Rainbow.

Man of the Rainbow. She was talking about Roz in that lifetime—Golden Winged Hawk.

I wonder if she will find him; we all need a rainbow.

And then she went to the children:

All the children...I tried to save them, but I couldn't. I couldn't help them.... I can't help anyone...I have to let go...I tried. Marda...she was so independent.... Running Deer...where is he? He's always running away.... When he comes, he makes me laugh. We were taken to the woods...the warriors...gone...our warriors...they're dragging me by my arm.

I saw her being pulled by the right arm. No wonder that arm has given her so much pain—she holds memory in the cells of her body.

Silver Eagle...oh God, the burden...

I have witnessed some of the most horrendous past-life and current-life regressions with clients, friends and family members without shedding a tear. But these tribal memories had begun to hit me harder. Yes, I had begun to feel more and see more. I saw my father, Silver Eagle—and again I knew the pain. I reached for another tissue, thankful that I did not need to speak at that moment.

DeLaine's focus moved back to her husband:

He is making himself sick; he doesn't want to stay. He hated what he did in that life (as a soldier)...he hates blood now, he can't stand the sight of blood...or feces. When the babies were little...he has so much anger, so much anger.

As DeLaine sensed her time of passing from that earlier lifetime, she recognized that much of the violence and revenge of the soldiers had been due to their own families having been killed by warring Indian tribes.

Before I brought her back into the room, I asked DeLaine to visualize the unborn infant that she had known and also her appearance as Lynette and send White Light energy and love to that soul. I then asked that she do the same with her husband and if she had any messages or thoughts that she wanted to communicate to them, to do it mentally and privately. After giving her time to do that, I brought her back into the room as we both reached for more tissues.

Dot and Robert

Not long after this regression with DeLaine, Dot's former husband, Robert, planned to come down for a visit. I had been eager to talk with him, to jog my memory of his experience in those early regressions that we had done. But two days before our scheduled discussion he called and said, "Janet, about my coming down to talk about the tribe, I've decided that I don't want to talk about it."

"What?" I could hardly believe what he was saying.

"I've decided that I don't want to talk about it," he repeated. "I want to live in the present and look to the future."

I had heard Dot voice a similar desire—to forget who she had been and what she had done in *this* life.

"Okaaay," I replied very slowly, "and you think that talking about that life for an hour is living in the past?"

Ignoring my comment and using a broken-record technique he repeated his decision. "I've decided I don't want to talk about it."

Whew! As far as my writing was concerned, I could manage without his talking to me—the capacity of my own memory has proven good enough both for me and for others. However, I felt disappointed not to have his support and surprised at his reaction.

"Robert, I need to ask you," I said, "do you have any problem with my writing this story?"

"No," he replied, "*I* don't." He seemed to be saying that someone else did. "You'll be writing it as fiction anyway," he added.

"Well, I'll be writing it as it actually happened in my life," I corrected him, "and changing the names and descriptions only of those people who prefer anonymity."

Several months earlier I had asked Robert if Anna would be willing to meet with me and he said he thought that she would. Even though they were no longer in a relationship, they maintained some contact and he seemed willing to introduce us—if she agreed. Robert had told me that Anna had attempted artificial insemination and now had a healthy baby. Because of what I knew of her past life in the tribe I understood her determination and need to have a baby. This fascinated me. Although Anna did not believe in reincarnation, I assumed she would not have a closed mind. I would have liked to have met her, but if Robert was not even willing to talk, I felt quite certain that meeting Anna would be out of the question.

Internally I asked myself. *Do I live in the past?* No, this was not even an issue for me. All of my past lives of which I am aware have helped me to understand who I am today. But the value of that information lies in recognizing its current effect and in moving through the blockages that hold me back. I have no current desire to be a monk in Tibet, or a nun in France, or chief of an American Indian tribe. I am quite happy with my life and with who I am and with my desire for further expansion and growth.

Not even talk about it? I remained puzzled by Robert's reaction. Perhaps he still had some issues from that earlier life, issues that he had not yet dealt with.

Again I repeated my question, asking if Robert had any problem with my writing the story, and again he said no, so I canceled our visit. We still planned to have lunch together the following week, something we had not done for a long time. But Kay called to cancel even that get-together—Robert had come down with the flu.

Meanwhile, Roz began painting White Fawn, his friend of that earlier lifetime. Karen posed for him in Native American dress from her shop. Kate had mailed Roz a photo of Judy DeGuzman, the woman who had been her mother and White Fawn's sister in the tribe. Roz's painting, therefore, would be a composite of several women from our group. I continued to feel amazed at how we assisted one another.

When I finally saw this painting, I was astounded. The technique that Roz used this time, realism, was entirely different from what he had done in his other paintings. It even looked as if it had been painted by a different artist. The beauty and spirituality of this painting prompted me to ask Roz if I could use it on the front of the book. Roz's painting of White Fawn had many facets. He and I commented on it. We saw:

Healing the earth
Rebirth of the tribe
Madonna and Child
Feminine energy being brought into the earth
Christ figure
A tribute to motherhood
Mother Earth being reborn
Tepees indicating a civilization of long ago
Strength of the Native American Indian woman
Healing through inner peace and meditation
God/Goddess energy
White Fawn healing herself...and her unborn fetus

Marda

Marda became the next member of our group to seek a regression. When she arrived at my office we both knew what memories she needed to re-live and release. Unlike other regressions, in which neither the client nor I knew what would happen, this time we were quite certain. Since the holidays Marda had experienced a time of settling of her unconscious memories. There had also been a time of releasing control and intensifying her emotions.

Between work and family obligations Marda had no private time to work through the things that had been told to her during the past six weeks. Even though she enjoyed her activities, she recognized her need for time alone. She was tired. Finally, in desperation, she told her husband that she needed a weekend away from everyone. He understood, and she made reservations at a hotel for the weekend to rest and recuperate from the persistent demands on her energy. She came to my office on Friday afternoon before she was to go away. The time was right.

Marda's experience became one of seeing and re-living rather than verbalizing. It is one thing to be told by a psychic about a past-life trauma; it is quite another thing to have one's own experience and memory. It seems that the strongest release takes place through one's own memory.

Marda relaxed and began to enter an altered state. The braces bothered her mouth. She began to twist, pull back in the chair, and finally to sob as she whispered softly.

> Marda: *...a gun in my mouth...oh...no...(More softly.) Go away.... (Crying.) ...I tried to scream—I can't...there's a gun in my mouth...and there are soldiers laughing...they're laughing...and I'm scared.... (Deep breaths and crying continued for a long time.)*
>
>   *He's on me again...everyone's laughing...(Deep breaths and crying.)...oh...oh...just let it be over, let it be over.... (Gasping to take in air.) ...Oh...oh...it's over.*
>
>   *When he's done, the others come up...and they have me...and I don't care...(Crying.)...I don't care anymore...I just want to go...after they have their fun, they stab me...(Raising her voice.) ...over and over and over! (Deep breaths.)*
>
> Janet: *How many men are there?*
>
> Marda: *I don't know...there's lots of them.*

Marda re-lived the experience, needing no guidance or input from me. A long time into the regression I asked:

> Janet: *Where were you? How did this happen?*
>
> Marda: *I was playing.... I was off by myself playing in the woods like I always did. I liked to be by myself. I had been there the day before, and I thought I saw something. I saw something...and when I went back that evening, I told everyone, but they wouldn't listen. So I thought I was making it up, too. So I went back again. And that was when they found me.... They were waiting for me. (She continued to take deep breaths.)*
>
>   *I tried to scream, and that was when they jammed the gun into my mouth. I tried to fight back, but I couldn't...I wasn't big enough...or strong...and that was when they had their fun.*
>
>   *When they were done I felt dead, but I wasn't dead...they kicked me around like a rag doll...and one of them decided to get rid of me...(Crying.)...they dug a hole...covered me with dirt...I was dead but not dead...*

(Very lightly whispering.)...just glad it was over...just hearing them going away...their laughter...talking about the next fun thing they could do.

I instructed her to feel her spirit release from the body.

Marda: *I'm glad...I'm glad I can go. Arms reaching out for me...welcoming me home...such a relief....*

For the first time since she had sat down in the chair Marda was in a peaceful state. I encouraged her to stay there for a few moments to feel the love and Light and safety. If she didn't go there on her own, I was prepared to move her into the childhood of her present life, but as it turned out I didn't need to give any instructions.

Marda: *I'm a baby in somebody's arms. I feel like I'm snuggled up at somebody's breast just like a baby; it feels so good.*
Janet: *Who is holding you?*
Marda: *(With surprise.) ...Grandmother.*

Again, I prepared to move Marda ahead in time. But as if our unconscious minds were connected, before I said the words she was there. She suddenly put her hands over her face and sobbed uncontrollably.

Marda: *Not again! Not again! Not again.... Oh...I can't...it's the same setting...I was playing by myself. Oh...my big brother...I trusted...*
Janet: *Is there anyone to help you?*
Marda: *No, no, nobody's there. I know it's not right...it's not just a game...it's not just a game...it's not a game, I know. (Crying.) Oh... (Deep breaths.)*
                I tried.... I kicked and I screamed and I ran, and I fell. Dad found me. He told me not to tell...not to say a word to anybody.
Janet: *How do you feel?*
Marda: *(Crying.) ...Angry, hurt.*
Janet: *What was it that your father told you?*

Marda: *Things are better left unsaid.... My mother would be too*
              upset.... Just do these things...just forget about it, it will go
              away. So I did. I never told anybody. I never wore the dress
              again. He (her brother) suffered all his life. I never knew.
              Every time he looked at me, he suffered. I never knew it.

Marda suddenly felt her brother's spirit presence in the room.

Marda: *He's here.*
Janet: *Yes, I know.*

We concluded the session by my encouraging Marda to speak privately with her brother, saying what she needed to communicate to him and hearing what he needed to communicate to her. I knew that forgiveness was taking place.

Marda: *He's free...and I'm free now.*

Dot Withdraws

As Marda and the other Circle members continued to heal, all of them encouraged me to write our story. The majority told me to use their real names so I was astonished when, a few days after having breakfast and a late gift exchange at Dot's house, I received a letter from her. This very close friend expressed upset that I had questioned something in a channeling session she had done for someone. She went on to say that she felt Standing Tree did not belong in the Silver Eagle story because too much remained hidden for me to portray her character accurately. She said that in trance she had recently "unraveled the karma of the tribe" but did not want to share this information with the others unless they asked her directly.
Portray Standing Tree's story? I had no intention of portraying Standing Tree's story—nor the stories of White Fawn or Running Deer or Little Feather. What was this about?
After working so closely for five years that we could almost read each other's minds, we found ourselves out of sync now. Obviously,

there were deeper issues involved, and if Dot did not want to be questioned she certainly didn't want *me* around.

As for Dot's psychic impressions of the karma of the tribe, I had long ago learned that any psychic impressions—whether through intuition, tarot, or any form of channeling—move through the human system. It cannot be any other way. As long as we are in a human body we "carry ourselves with us." All of the members of our Circle had worked for years in clearing ourselves of blockages to vision, but we would *always* be subject to our own human perceptions through the veils that exist. Whether we look to astral projection, akashic readings, or any other source, we still take ourselves—our consciousness—with us.

Just as we take our consciousness with us, we also come to tune in to one another. Thus it had become common now for members of our group to know when another experienced trouble. It should not have surprised me, then, when Michael called and asked, "So, Janet, what's wrong?"

I shared what had taken place with Robert and also the letter I had received from Dot and said, "It's bizarre. With our entire group, only two people have pulled back support or mentioned any hesitation at all about my writing the story—and they are two of the people who went away to the cave in that life. Is that a coincidence? This sounds ridiculous, but I feel as if I'm repeating something that Silver Eagle did—he gave them his blessing when they went away to the cave. This is strange."

The process of moving from a position of powerlessness to one of power involves confusion while we learn our parameters and what *true power* is. I wondered if all of us simply "continued where we left off" in following through with some soul experiences. I tried to look inside myself to separate my feelings from the sure knowledge that each of us must follow his own path. I wanted to act in love with that understanding.

I remembered years ago when Dot, with great emotion, had asked, "How can I ever trust Robert again?!"

"You need to trust Robert to do what is right for Robert," was my very unwelcome reply.

Dot reminded me that I had also told her that some day she would thank Anna. At the time she said she had felt like throwing something at me. Only years later did she recognize that when Robert had followed his path, her own had changed. "I do thank Anna," she said. "I'm happier and more whole than I've ever been in my life."

Whatever was occurring now, we needed to allow space for healing to take place. I knew that Dot and Robert were doing what they needed to do; I anticipated that same kind of understanding from them.

Deb's Memories

Setting this matter aside to heal, I wanted to talk with Deb Nelsen again about her memories. Deb and I made arrangements to meet at Scott's apartment in Elmira after she finished her shift at the hospital. Warnings of a six-inch snowfall pushed me out of my place early in the morning to get to Elmira before the heavy snow arrived. I made it just in time. Deb telephoned to say that she would be there for our get-together in spite of weather conditions. Heavy snow would have been a deterrent to *me*—not to Deb. *I could benefit from a dose of her strength* I thought as I hung up the phone.

Deb Nelson's powerful personality and strength covers the incredible sensitivity of this woman. I have known her to stop two lanes of traffic to pick up a dog that had been hit and then drive to a vet and pay bills for its care while she began to search for the owner. Her love and caring for animals and for the earth holds no bounds. I have also watched her give to and care for friends in a way for which most of us do not have the capacity. Circle members encouraged her to give that same kind of nurturing attention to herself.

Deb lay down on the large bed and made herself comfortable. Her long straight dark hair covered the pillow beneath her head. In preparation for going into trance to bring forward clear information, Deb had readied herself the previous day through bodywork with DeLaine and fasting. Deb's preparation, we discussed later, proved to be valuable in that she seemed to be in movement among three dimensions at the same time: aware that she was in trance state talking with me, perceiving and remembering that Indian lifetime, and also speaking from a Higher-Self perspective. There were times, she said later, that she felt as if a part of her mind could have spoken in the dialect of the time. At other times she felt as if she were "translating" in order to answer my questions. She began by seeing herself in a lovely, peaceful setting.

Deb:	*I see myself standing on a mountaintop, beautiful billowy clouds, blue sky, the sun is shining.*
Janet:	*Good...move your energy more into your body in that time and space, and describe your body to me.*
Deb:	*Very masculine...very broad shoulders, intricate beadwork on cuffs on shoulders. I can see my horse right next to me, just standing there. Starburst, that's his name, beautiful paint. (Laughing.) ...It's like a dog. It's following me all over, just nudging me, very playful, very loving animal.*
Janet:	*Feel yourself in that time and space, and tell me, how are you feeling on this day?*
Deb:	*I see vehicles of transport coming across.*

What an unusual way for Deb to describe what she was seeing, I thought.

Janet:	*Tell me about these vehicles.*
Deb:	*Round, wooden slats on sides, white pillows on top.*
Janet:	*What are you thinking as you see these vehicles of transport?*
Deb:	*I see horses pulling them.*
Janet:	*Have you ever seen these before?*
Deb:	*No.*
Janet:	*How do you feel as you watch this?*
Deb:	*I feel my face going...(Showing confusion.) ...asking what are they doing? Where are they going?*
Janet:	*Tell me, are you alone, or is anyone with you?*
Deb:	*I'm alone.*
Janet:	*Do you come to this place often?*
Deb:	*To meditate, to give my prayers. The Great Spirit and I are one.*

Janet: *Can you tell me approximately how old are you?*

I sensed an immediate confusion about my question...she/he did not know what I was talking about when I asked about age.

Deb: *I do not know your meaning of...I am very skilled...I have children....*
Janet: *Can you tell me about your children?*
Deb: *A young boy. He plays with the other children...has not learned skills of the woods, the hillsides...not a warrior yet. Fine son. I have a baby daughter, in the arms....*

Deb seemed to lift in awareness as she said:

Deb: *Maybe that is why I'm on this hillside. I see my wife, she is very beautiful.*
Janet: *Can you tell me the name of your wife? What do you call her?*
Deb: *Sun...sun...*
Janet: *Okay, let it go for right now, it will come. Can you tell me any more about your family? Where are they?*
Deb: *We are very happy, at peace...peace.... Things are coming across...we are very concerned.... I do not feel good about them.*

I directed Deb to move ahead to the next significant event, whether that event be minutes, hours, days, weeks, or years later. Unlike the anger that I remembered years ago when Flaming Arrow had spoken, this time I heard a subdued voice and a soul-sadness.

Deb: *Something is happening, definitely...half of the tribe is gone...there is fire, there is smoke...there is—I have just come onto such mass confusion.*
Janet: *Where are you, what are you doing?*
Deb: *I'm standing there in awe, I cannot move. There is...gone. I had been sent out to see where these people with white skin are coming from, with a group of three others. We have been gone for many days. We came back...to see this.*
Janet: *Tell me, what do you see?*

Deb:	Crying, moaning, chanting, dead bodies, the tribe is much smaller.
Janet:	What has happened here? What has happened to your people?
Deb:	Someone has attacked us.
Janet:	Who has done this?
Deb:	I can hear our cry—the spirit. How could we have...? Why has this happened? Why have they done this? We never hurt anyone. We...live in peace, we were very happy.
Janet:	What of your family? What has happened to them?
Deb:	They've...they've been killed, slaughtered. (Her mind moved to a different place.) I'm back up on the hill. I am told more to come.
Janet:	How do you feel now?
Deb:	(Speaking with anger.) How dare they take this land! They will ravage it. Fight. (Then she whispers.) How could they have done this?
Janet:	How can you fight?
Deb:	Our warriors are gone. There were four, four that were with me. (Smiling.) ...They left us the crazy woman.[5]
Janet:	Tell me about her.
Deb:	She's over...singing...senseless. She's still very here. I'm near water. I see that there's a lake, but I do not...there's moving water by it. I do not see the stillness of it. This is June...planting time, little leaves are on trees, little growth.
Janet:	Will your people do any planting this time?
Deb:	No.
Janet:	What will become of you?
Deb:	We will move on, foraging. There are so very few to hunt.

I asked Deb to move ahead in time on the count of three.

Deb:	Council fires. Silver Eagle says, "We cannot fight...these... people. We must offer them peace and hope that we may stay as a tribe, so that our blood may move like a spring, that we may see the next moon...and our children find happiness and peace that we have in Mother Earth."

Deb again lifted to a more conscious state while still seeing.

Deb: *I'm sitting there as Flaming Arrow, in disgust.*

Again, she dropped in consciousness.

Deb: *Heyokah Cayote says, "I am right behind you. You will be
              warned...and heed the call. The sun...will be covered by
              the moon...and the wolf will howl...a song of goodbye."
              (With deep sadness.) We will **not** sit in council...ever again.
              Silver Eagle is shaking his head. There are only six...seven
              of us, sitting around. (Change in facial expression.)*
Janet: *What is it?*
Deb: *The tribe is so small. Women are cowered like dogs in a
              cage. We were all so happy. It will never be the same. What
              did we do to change this? We took our meat in the sacred
              manner. We offered prayers to the spirits and our guides
              and always to the four directions.... What is this message?*

              *We are doomed. We are doomed...to the onslaught of
              these creatures...(Voice filled with disgust.)...called White!
              Where are their women? I do not see the women! There is
              no balance in their lives!*

              *I remember the story of the grandfathers, telling us of
              a big Shake of Mother Earth...and the earth trembled, and
              the rocks would fall...and the animals and their people
              were so afraid...just as a horse shaking itself off to loosen
              the dirt. These people...they keep coming.... They have no
              regard for life. They have no understanding of the medicine
              of the Oglala...nor of the grandfathers. They cannot take
              without giving back. They must remember...to love yourself
              in order to love your brothers and your sisters. There is to
              be a big change. I do not understand why.*
Janet: *What is this change that is coming?*
Deb: *The earth is shaking, is off-balance.... The change, the
              earth...is to change, we have heard that. Don't be fooled
              that there is an easy way out. The work must be done. The
              tribe will be gone. The tribe will be back.*

Moving ahead in time...

Deb: *The wolves are calling...the wolves are calling...we heard
              it in the wind. The tribe is decimated, chopped, scattered.*

> *I can feel the hatred...anger...fear...and sorrow...and I'm aware of the feelings. They butchered! They can take my life but they can't take my soul! (With deep emotion and tears rising.) I cannot love these people. (Deep breaths and tears.) We were such a proud people. I cannot love these people. I cannot...I don't know how to....*

I moved Deb to the end of that life.

Deb: *I am with my family, Sunburst is at my side...times of passion...playing with the children.*

It became apparent that Flaming Arrow was connecting with his spirit instead of the physical body. The next words explained why.

Deb: *I...I cannot see...because I am blindfolded. My eyes are covered with a cloth. This is the end.*

Janet: *Can you tell me more?*

Deb: *I'm passing...we are passing. We will not be forgotten. Our passing has connected us...layer upon layer...as it expands out...touching each other...playing games, laughing and singing. We need to laugh more. Silver Eagle was so proud of his tribe. The sadness of the passing...is not so sad...anymore. There is a feeling of understanding. It is not...what our tribe needed...we were just caught up in the chaos. The sadness of the massacre...we will remember. He's looking down—I'm looking down.*

Janet: *And as you look down, what do you see?*

Deb: *Blue jacket, fire stick, laughing...a new form of laughter. I spit on them! These men are **terrible**...to do this to me. I smell a smell...flesh...and an odor I do not recognize.... I know now that it's alcohol. (Speaking slowly and with much confusion.) I can not describe...these people...or compare them...because there is nothing to compare them with. They do not behave like any I have **ever** seen! I know every tree and branch, buffalo, flowers, the badger, the bear...maybe like a lizard...but even lizards have worth. I feel the pain and presence of the tribe. My family is just a dream.*

Janet: *Tell me the last thing you see before you pass over.*

Deb: *I see myself hanging. My hands are bound. I have pain in my left leg. The fire stick. No! I cannot!*

The warrior energy of Flaming Arrow is back, I thought. Deb's regression seemed to put me back on my path after the experience of Dot and Robert's withdrawals. I began to think about my upcoming trip.

Chapter XIII

Preparing to Remember: Late January 1991

Margaret

Before I left for Florida, where I planned to begin writing about
the tribe, I contacted a number of the people who had regressed to
lifetimes in the tribe in order to tie up loose ends and obtain material
I would need. First, my son Scottie and I made a trip to Maryland to
visit Sara.[6] I hoped, also, to talk with Margaret Osborne, the woman
who had been Silver Eagle's other mate in that lifetime. Sara lives
about two hours from Margaret and we were not able to get together,
but I did talk with her by phone.

Margaret is a woman of "mothering energy" who, like DeLaine,
is quite capable and in control of any situation. We had never done
a regression to the Indian incarnation and she said that she did not
have personal memories, but Sara had seen her as one of Silver
Eagle's mates. Margaret said that she did recognize her name from
an Indian incarnation to be Rising Sun, and that name is important
to her now. She had recently taken a shield-making workshop in the
Native American tradition. In meditation she had seen a symbol of
the sun and had put that on her shield.

Gradually I found that not only had the members of the tribe
come forward to this current lifetime but so had many of the soldiers
who had been our attackers. When I arrived back home from the visit
with Sara, I found that two of the women in our Circle were going

147

through turmoil with their husbands. Though the couples lived in different towns, both husbands had begun to express a strong possessiveness and anger that surprised and frustrated their wives. I listened as each wife described by phone what sounded like very real power struggles. During each conversation I felt an urge to yell, "Don't let them kill you again!"

I kept my mouth shut, stayed in the counselor mode, and observed this strange reaction of my mind. Neither of these women was in any physical danger and I am not accustomed to such melo-dramatic thought. I understood this related not to physical but more to a mental and emotional danger that stems from giving up one's power to another person. I sensed that the husbands of both of these women had been soldiers in the earlier lifetime. Their unconscious need to make amends may have been surfacing as possessiveness.

Dan

As I moved closer to writing this story, I felt a need to visit my son Dan to learn his memories of the tribe and of his life as Flying Arrow. Dan had moved from Boston to the Midwest and I soon found myself on a plane to see him. My other son, Scottie, had seen an image of his brother as an Indian wearing a headdress and carrying arrows on his back. He had also seen feathers mounted for a wing-like effect on this Indian's arms. "I just saw Dan!" he had exclaimed.

My visit with Dan was most enjoyable. His ability to flow with the happenings around him once prompted a friend to nickname him "Reed in the River of Life." One afternoon I started to describe the Indian that Scottie had seen in meditation. No sooner had I mentioned the headdress when Dan described the rest. "It was me!" he said. "The headdress was a half-mask like a hawk and came down to the nose. I always had arrows on my back. I can see it as clear as anything."

Dan is one of those people for whom altered states of consciousness are normal. This is not uncommon in creative people who use their right brain freely. Dan's psychic "knowing" is as strong as that of any client with whom I have worked and I am relieved that he is also well-grounded. He rejects extremes in the New Age movement as much as I (and most other members of our tribe) do. He easily moved himself into an hypnotic state and I suggested that he go to the lifetime in the tribe of Silver Eagle, "...if in fact you were there."

Dan saw fire inside a tepee and a campsite and friendly familiar faces. It was a comfortable feeling; he sensed Robert and others. He spent much time on rocks on a small mountain top where he saw himself in dance—slow rhythmic movements similar to those of Tai Chi. A hawk would appear flying and encircling him and he recognized the hawk to be his animal spirit guide.

Dan: *There was such a good feeling there, felt like such purpose—my job on the mountain. I was a medicine man of some sort. There was an older man in the beginning, sitting watching me use my arms and flowing. He didn't talk. He had grey hair tied back and a wrinkled face. Eventually I went on my own. The hawk was always there. When I came down from the hill Brian would often meet me and we would walk to camp. We were excited about what we were doing. I see a female, perhaps a mate, with long black hair and a dress over her knees.*

   I saw myself at night dancing around a fire wearing the half mask. I had hawk or eagle feathers on the sides of my arms and would spread my arms and dance. Each person's headdress or outfit represented him in some way.

Dan saw himself being sent out as a scout.

Dan: *I was sitting on a horse looking at Silver Eagle as he sent four of us out. I felt so proud and have such good feelings when I remember the chief. Riding was bareback, racing and hanging onto the mane with a strong grip. We broke off and met over the hill, spread out so we couldn't talk but could signal to each other. We were crawling up on a hill and I motioned for someone to go tell the tribe. The one*

who went back to tell the tribe was younger. I don't know
if he made it or not.

Dan recognized that his death occurred quickly. Someone came
up behind him, threw a rope around his neck, and he was dragged by
a horse.

Dan: *It happened quick. The hawk was ready to take me,*
              circling... as a hawk circled, I kept circling up.

After Dan's experience he told me that the image of himself on
the high rock doing slow arm movements while staring into the eyes
of a hawk had come to him before spontaneously while driving, as he
had listened to a piece of music by Pink Floyd. Whenever he heard
that music, the same image came to his mind—the hawk's eyes and
the feeling that he could connect with the hawk and fly. A few years
later Dan bought a cassette tape by Pink Floyd and recognized the
music. "I'll play it for you," he said now as he found the cassette and
slipped it into his stereo. I had to admit that the music would *not*
have brought to my mind the image that Dan described. "Look at the
title," he said as he pointed to the cassette case. I was astonished as
I read the words: "Learning to Fly."[7]

This visit with Dan preceded final preparations for my trip to
Naples to write. I remembered that long *before* the painting of Silver
Eagle had arrived at my house I had regressed three separate
people—Dot, Robert and Deb—to the same Indian tribe and had
recorded those sessions. Now Dot and Robert did not wish to share
their recordings.

Deb

Deb, however, agreed to loan me her tape. I remembered the
strong warrior energy that had come through her voice and
remembered, also, her anger. Deb's tape arrived by mail and I
appreciated her willingness to share it with me. I sat down and began
to listen. At first she had spoken of an island lifetime but when I had

moved her to "a memory that is affecting you now," her happy, pleasant voice took on a heavy, aggressive tone. I felt shocked to hear something that I had completely forgotten—this had taken place *before* the painting of Silver Eagle had arrived, before Robert's regression, and before we had gained all the information about our tribe that we now understood. The date was September 2, 1986.

Deb:	*I see a red man, baiting these people to come out of this cave. I hear Flaming Arrow over and over again. He's saying, "Come out, come out. We need you, we need you." (Pause.) He is me.*
	I have leggings on. "There's strength in number." I'm at the mouth of a cave with a little rock on this side and a big rock on the other side as you're looking in. I see some faces. There's a big argument going on.
Janet:	*Tell me about the argument.*
Deb:	*The person I'm arguing with is saying, "We are weak, we are tired." He's got a stick in his hand to kind of pull himself up. We can't fight anymore.*
Janet:	*Do you know who this person is?*
Deb:	*He has a thin strip of rawhide in his hair...I hear a lot of crying...(Imitated a moaning sound.)...not crying, but like moaning. (Sadly.) I am walking away.*
Janet:	*What is your feeling?*
Deb:	*Disgust. I just went like this....(Making a throw-back motion with her arm.) Stay here!*
Janet:	*Why are you disgusted with them?*
Deb:	*I'm crying now.*
Janet:	*Your disgust has turned to tears?*
Deb:	*Yes, I'm crying now 'cause I know it's near the end. Don't...I'm saying to myself, "Don't cry." Very dry...no food, no water, I feel real hungry. Parched mouth.*
Janet:	*Where are the others? Not in the cave...where are the others?*
Deb:	*Hanging in trees. It's like one big line. There's four or five...I can't count them, I can't look at them. I'm looking down at a yellow-haired man with a blue suit, a blue cavalry outfit on. He's laughing at me, poking me with his gun.*
Janet:	*How do you feel toward him?*
Deb:	*I spit on him.*

Deb's conscious mind became more alert as she said to me, "I'm just fighting this really heavy.... It's like I keep going in and out of it...I don't really want to see it. I'm spinning around."

I sensed the struggle of Deb's mind. Obviously this lifetime was a powerful one for her, yet it didn't seem that she could continue or go deeper into that experience during her regression. I moved Deb into higher levels of consciousness where she could evaluate her experiences and see their effects on her.

Deb: *Oh God, so much hate.*

I asked her to tell me if she recognized anyone from that life who was with her now.

Deb: *I don't know, I couldn't look at them. I just glanced at the bodies hanging. I couldn't look.*

Before bringing Deb back into the room, I asked if there were any thoughts that came from her Higher Self.

Deb: *Forgive them, for they know not what they do.*

Preparation through Bodywork

Hearing Deb's regression experience once again, I felt prepared for my trip to Florida. I knew that while visiting Michael and Kate I would try to put myself into an altered state to look at my own lifetime in the Silver Eagle tribe. I needed to have my own experience. *What would I see?* I knew that I had been the last to die before my father. *Would I be able to reach that lifetime? What would I remember?*

In a phone call with Michael, he said, "You make it sound like we're going to put you on a bed of nails. We also have the sun, the beach, a pleasant atmosphere, peace and quiet." *He was right, the trip would be a vacation. So why this inner turmoil?*

Shortly before leaving I followed my intuition to call John Perestam, the chiropractor where Marda worked. To my surprise I got an appointment to see him before I left for Florida. I told him about my hand going numb at night and then admitted, "I'm really here because my intuition told me that I needed to come to you." When he began to work on me I realized how valuable my instincts had been.

"Dr. John" is a true healer. For some time now I'd had a visual image that I had moved my heart "back and to the right" so as to "protect" it. The doctor began by checking the muscles in my left arm and he recognized immediately why my arm had been going numb. Some adjustments remedied that. Next he checked my body, especially the heart area, and mentioned "heart issues." He shook his head and said, "Your heart is out of position, moved back and to the right slightly, held out of place by ribs." I could hardly believe my ears. I had actually manifested my unconscious fears, manifested them into my physical body![8] He did some more adjustments and for the first time in weeks I could breathe naturally.

Next I needed to see DeLaine for bodywork but it had snowed the night before my appointment and I looked out my apartment window that morning thinking that perhaps the roads would be too slippery. But the roads had cleared and traffic moved normally. Was it a touch of disappointment that I felt?

Yet another part of me looked forward to being on DeLaine's massage table; there was no question that I needed the bodywork. *I never used to be late*, I thought, as I heard over the car radio that it was after 10:00 A.M. I had left my apartment in plenty of time. Scraping ice off the car windows, stopping at my office to turn on the answering machine, and automatically heading east on the expressway instead of west—all of these things made me wonder if DeLaine needed some space before I arrived. But I was wrong. As I realized later, my own unconscious had caused this stalling.

As my car turned into DeLaine's driveway I looked out across the field and remembered one day when Dan and his cousin Ginger were little and we had visited the farm. DeLaine's husband told them that years ago Indians roamed this land. Dan and Ginger grew excited and rushed out to search for arrowheads. I smiled at this memory.

Dan—Flying Arrow—naturally was the only one in years to find an arrowhead on this land.

When I arrived in DeLaine's office we first spent some time catching up on each other's experiences. Things had begun to happen so quickly in our own lives and those of people around us that they called for extensive catch-up time.

"What are we going to do today?" she asked.

I made myself comfortable on the massage table and told her, "I have no idea. Just use your intuition."

I never felt the tightness in my neck until DeLaine's hands touched me—always in the right spot. "Silver Eagle is here with a message," she said as I felt her move into a trance state and channel with her hands still on my head. Through DeLaine, Silver Eagle spoke to me about letting myself feel as the memories came to me.

> Silver Eagle: Your training was strong...I trained you to use your mind," he said as I again remembered myself walking with him. "Now you must allow yourself to feel the memories...and with the feeling, the creativity floods open. The dam that you have built is so high, so strong, as of concrete. A small opening so as to trickle out will not do...the dam must break...and Michael is the one to break the dam.

"I trust he will do it softly," I joked.

Only a few days earlier I had written to Michael that whenever I pictured myself in Florida I saw myself crying. *I don't cry easily,* I thought. *Why do I see myself crying so much and so hard?*

"I know that Michael is the one," I said to Silver Eagle through DeLaine. "But why is it Michael?"

Tears came to my eyes as Silver Eagle replied:

> Because you see yourself in Michael.

"Oh God...I don't want to feel that much!" I exclaimed.

> Silver Eagle: And there was a friendship with Running Deer that was lost. Lifetime after lifetime you have lost people whom

*you loved. When you gave your heart, so many times they
were taken away. That is why it is so easy for you to detach
now...you had to learn to go on. And it is why you keep
people at a distance when it comes to your heart.*

*When the memories come—and we do not say when
they will come—stay with the pictures, stay with the feeling.*

"I don't know if I can," I said, trying to imagine myself maintaining an emotional state that I had never reached before, never allowed before. Consciously I felt willing to do that—go through the memories so I could move beyond them and free myself, free my own creativity. But I had long ago learned that the training of my unconscious mind was much stronger—it had an automatic shut-off valve that kicked in when it came to feeling emotion for an extended period.

DeLaine completed the channeling segment. She shook herself back to a more reality-based place and sipped from a glass of water, removing her shoes to ground herself more. "I'm being told that I need to help open your heart," she said. "I'll hold my hand over your heart for a period of time until either you or I feel that it is time to remove it."

Her hand held comforting warmth as she placed it directly on my chest. Within seconds she let out a gasp and clapped her other hand over her mouth. "Are you seeing anything?" she asked. I wasn't but I was more than aware DeLaine could see something.

"Just say what you can see, DeLaine," I told her, knowing that at this point she could not stop the pictures. DeLaine kept her right hand on my chest as her left hand grabbed her own stomach and she screamed, *"They cut out your heart...they cut out your heart...and gave it to Silver Eagle!!!"*

I could not see these pictures, but tears flooded my eyes. DeLaine struggled, telling herself, "Stay with it, stay with it...." and kept her hand over my heart.

That night I wrote to Michael and told him what DeLaine had perceived. A few days later the phone rang and a soft male voice said, "I'm breaking a vow."

"You're breaking a vow?" I asked. "What vow is that?"

"To not call you, due to fiscal responsibility," Michael said, "but you can't send a letter like that and not expect to hear from me."

"Do you think that actually happened?" I asked. I was anxious to know his response.

With emphatic voice he replied, "Every part of my being says that it is right. I *know* that it's accurate. I know that what DeLaine saw was real." I wondered what further horrors I would see when I sat down with Michael to look for myself.

Before leaving town I felt a desire to connect with several people from the tribe who had been especially close to me in this life. First I met with DeLaine and Marda, and Deb called to give encouragement and support.

Soon after this I joined Elaine for breakfast. We caught up on each other's lives, and I asked her if she wanted me to use a fictitious name when I wrote about the tribe. She hadn't realized that she would be included in the writing, since as a baby she had few memories. At first she said to use her name and then after thinking about it decided that for family reasons a different name should be used. I asked her about her comment at the Celebration party, about "not shaming the tribe." She said when she heard it come out of her mouth she thought that it sounded rather dramatic. I speculated that as the baby she picked up messages from the people around her, and one message was to be proud, to be strong, and to not disgrace ourselves or one another. When she had made the statement that evening I felt that she spoke straight from her own unconscious based on messages that she had absorbed.

I called Vickie next. She said she recently realized that as Wildflower she had not suffered Alzheimer's or senility in her old age. "My psychic energy was used up," she said. "It explains why I am so guarded in this life." I understood what she was saying, and her view corresponded with some of my research in obesity with highly sensitive people and their unconscious blockages.

I had lunch with Karen. She said to use her name in my writing. "I'm so happy that you are writing it as it really happened and not writing it as fiction," she added. "As you write it in this way, you empower every person in the tribe."

Karen's encouragement and that of many others moved me toward an increasing desire to tell the story of the tribe. At the same time I wanted to stay in hiding. No question about it, fear continued to rise inside me. I had deliberately kept my business small; I still did not advertise that I did past-life regressions. But living apart from Scott now, I had to assume more of my financial obligations. I felt as if I had put myself into a situation where I had to push myself in spite of myself.

Over a cup of coffee with Roz I expressed my concerns. "I realize that I'm dealing with unconscious fears, but when this story is told I'm afraid of being 'attacked' again." We talked about how quick people are to judge others and to scorn something that is different from their own belief system and/or experience. I had seen the media portray belief in reincarnation or the so-called "New Age" events in such an outrageous manner that I did not want to be pigeonholed in that way. I went on to say, "I'll no longer be seen as a traditional therapist."

Roz laughed in amazement. "Janet," he said, "you have never been a traditional therapist."

Chapter XIV

Heather Views the Massacre:
Early February 1991

I completed the last session of my seminar on "Relationships—the Challenge of Unconditional Love," and the next morning Roz drove me to the airport to fly to Naples.

During the flight my mind drifted back to a working weekend at least four years earlier that I had spent with Dot and a psychic friend. A drawing of a weary Indian on horseback had brought a spontaneous memory to Dot. As she saw herself as Standing Tree she sobbed, and this release of tears proved healing. Afterward the psychic (who was neither a member of our Circle nor of the tribe) went into trance and spoke directly to me, saying that the spirits of our tribe had not been released. In a sing-song voice she chanted over and over:

> *Wisdom Chief Child: Bury the dead, bury the dead.*
> *Wisdom Chief Child: Bury the dead, bury the dead.*
> *Wisdom Chief Child: Bury the dead, bury the dead.*

We made an attempt to connect with that life and with the massacre, but my unconscious mind had remained blocked against feeling emotions or bringing forward my own memories. I did not shed a tear nor could I remember that lifetime on my own. The psychic could see mental pictures of the chief and me hanging and said:

158

*Look at your father...what do you say to your father? What
words do you say to your father?*

I tried to cooperate but my mind refused to allow the memory. I
searched inside but the only words that came to me were, "They'll
never get to me."

I gazed out the window of the plane. So much had happened
since that time. I wondered if my pain were still too great for me to
re-live, but one thing felt certain—if I could not reach it with
Michael, I would not be able to reach it with anyone.

Michael met me at the airport. I stowed my winter coat in his car
and felt the warm sun on my body. "What beautiful weather Naples
has in February," I observed. We drove quickly to their town house,
and then Michael and Kate and I fell into a deep conversation.

Heather

The next day Heather Curtis joined us for dinner. She and I had
not been in touch since the previous summer and it was good to see
her again. As before, I was struck by a strength of presence that
manifested in her body size and energy, and I delighted in her sense
of humor, casual attire, and personality. In addition to her power, this
time I could see underlying anger and sorrow. She had changed jobs,
moved to Naples, and now lived only a few miles away.

After her initial visit Heather and I had not made contact again
except for brief phone calls. Both Kate and Michael said that she was
avoiding me.

"Avoiding me? Why?"

"Heather thinks that you can see inside of her," Kate answered.

"What makes her say that?" I asked.

Michael replied, "I see you do it."

It was possible that my presence affected Heather in some way.
I felt pleased when the next Sunday, at Kate's encouragement,
Heather came over to talk about it. Kate gently nudged Heather to
get into the discussion. "I realize I've been avoiding you," she said
finally as she looked directly into my eyes from her seat across the

patio table. "I don't know why. I know you're not going to push me, and yet..."

I began to fill in with some of my thoughts. "There is a lot going on at an unconscious level that we are not aware of," I said. "I have been told that I push people's unconscious minds in ways that I don't fully understand." We kept talking and I encouraged her to continue her spiritual path in the way that is right for her, not attempt to follow someone else's way. Heather is a social person, with lots of energy and she tires of the kind of spiritual talk that Kate, Michael, and I can do ad infinitum.

"It seems," I continued, "that there is an underlying similarity among all of us in the tribe. Perhaps it is true of everyone at this point in our evolution, but I am aware of some factors that characterize each of us—issues of power versus powerlessness and power versus love. Each of us is moving from feelings of powerlessness to power in love."

We continued our talk over cheese and crackers as Heather expressed her feelings of the past several days. With Michael and Heather a sense of humor underlies any discussion. We all felt better after talking together and Heather was the first to say, "Now can we go do something?" It was an easy transition and break from our mental work to swim suits and the beach for the afternoon. The warm sun, salty air, and joking relaxed us.

Heather, a photographer, suggested taking some photos of me to update those I had used during past years for my brochure and publicity. We hurriedly drove back from the beach and she gave me thirty minutes to shower, find something to wear between Kate's clothes and what I had packed in one bag, wash and dry my hair, and "get glamorous." Using two cameras and switching between black and white and color film she took several shots.

After dinner and an extended phone call from all of us to Roz back in New York, I joined the others who were in Kate's room looking through some of her books. I sat on the bed beside Heather, who had been comfortably lying down. To my surprise, the conversation moved to the possibility of Heather doing a regression. She said that in addition to her fear of the experience itself, she also harbored a concern that she wouldn't get anything.

I understood and said, "No problem. If nothing comes, that's okay." I told her that she could think about it and do it the next day, but the three others agreed that Heather was now relaxed, and if she waited she would build up resistance. It was late and I felt tired. *Am I up for this now?* I wondered, but I didn't want to miss this chance. Kate and Michael disappeared downstairs as I explained to Heather more about the process.

"Do you want to tape record it?" I asked. "It's up to you."

"We might as well," she replied. "If I do get something I might want to listen to it again."

Even though I felt curious to learn about her memories of the tribe, I knew that she might have had experiences in this life or other lifetimes that her mind needed to review. I decided that her personal healing was more important than the writing that I was doing. So, as usual, I gave no suggestions, other than to "go to the memory or experience that is most affecting you now."

Janet:	*Tell me, Heather, anything that you are sensing, feeling, or perceiving.*
Heather:	*My heart pounding.*
Janet:	*Okay, move your attention into your heart, move into that part of your body, and as you do that, just allow the memory to come. Why is your heart pounding?*
Heather:	*Fear. I'm hot.*
Janet:	*Okay, now I want you to gradually sense the space around you, the environment. Are you inside or outside?*
Heather:	*Outside.*
Janet:	*Are you alone, or with someone?*
Heather:	*(Whispering.) Alone, but there is someone watching.*
Janet:	*Okay, now I want you to move deeper and deeper into the experience; just let yourself be there. Is it daytime or nighttime?*
Heather:	*Sunset.*
Janet:	*Can you tell me more about where you are?*
Heather:	*Big field, it's all golden. There's a row of trees on the right side of me and I'm looking out across the field. The sun's making everything golden and the field's all glowing and it's okay, but I know there's somebody watching.*

Janet:	*Can you tell me what you are wearing on your feet, if anything?*
Heather:	*Nothing.*
Janet:	*Moving on up your body, what are you wearing?*
Heather:	*Some kind of pants.*
Janet:	*Continuing to move up your body, are you wearing anything on your upper body?*
Heather:	*No.*
Janet:	*Are you male or female?*
Heather:	*Male.*
Janet:	*Moving up to your face, your hair, tell me whatever comes.*
Heather:	*I do have a band around my head and my hair is dark.*
Janet:	*Can you tell me the color of your skin?*
Heather:	*Brown.*
Janet:	*Moving deeper and deeper into the experience, just allow yourself to be there. Tell me, how do you know that someone is watching you?*
Heather:	*I feel them, they're back behind me. I'm not scared, it's just that there's someone there.*
Janet:	*Do you feel comfort or danger with this?*
Heather:	*Seems okay, but it's uneasy, I can't tell. I want to be there, I want to be alone there, but there's someone watching.*
Janet:	*Can you tell me what you are doing in this place.*
Heather:	*Seems like I just want to be alone. I want to be there and look out into the field and say goodbye to the sun for the day, but someone's there looking; I don't know who it is.*

I moved Heather ahead in time within the same lifetime.

Heather:	*I have food, I was hunting and I'm bringing back something, a skin like fur, and I'm bringing it back.*
Janet:	*How do you feel about this?*
Heather:	*Good, but I was bad… (Laughing.) because I took too long watching the sun.*
Janet:	*Where are you going, where are you taking this?*
Heather:	*To the village. There's people around. I can see the tepees as clear as day. It's daytime now.*
Janet:	*Can you tell me more about what you see.*
Heather:	*They're laughing at me. (Heather laughs.) They're making fun of me 'cause I always go out to hunt and come back*

too late 'cause I wait till...I daydream. They caught me daydreaming a lot. It's okay, they're laughing and I'm laughing with them.

Janet: *Can you tell me more about what you see around you?*

Heather: *I see young children with the mothers and they seem to be playing something, they're happy; there's a lot of happiness. It's good. Seems to be kind of in a valley, there's a ridge of trees up on the hill, there's some horses tied up at the top of the hill.*

Janet: *Okay, as you bring the fur in, tell me what you do.*

Heather: *They're hanging it. It's small, maybe a coyote or something small, it hurts to have to kill it. I brought it back, I killed it, but I don't remember killing it. They're putting the skin up so we can use that. Seems calm, everybody seems happy, there's song, song around.*

Janet: *Good, can you tell me any more about what you are doing?*

Heather: *Just have to clean the hide hanging up on the clearing. Up on the top of that hill where the horses are, there's an X, you know, make the wood go in an X (Heather indicated with her hands how the wood was positioned.) to hang the hide on it to dry it right. There's bright light behind it, so it's still good daylight out there. There are other men around. I seem young, I don't...younger than they, they seem to be kidding, like they know I was gone awhile, but...*

Janet: *Approximately how old are you?*

Heather: *I'd say teenage, teen....*

Janet: *Okay.*

Heather: *I see things on my arms, on each arm there's a band.*

Janet: *Does it represent anything in particular?*

Heather: *They seem to be deer, deer skin, deer hide, maybe something I first caught, I don't know.*

I again moved Heather in time, to the "next significant event."

Heather: *I'm aware of my chest so heavy, and it's not pounding like it was, but it's heavy.*

Janet: *Why do you have a heaviness in your chest?*

Heather: *I don't know...I can feel...seems to be nighttime. I'm inside now, though. There's fire. I feel fur, like I'm sitting on...soft.*

Janet: *Okay. Who else is in this place with you?*

Heather: *There's some people, seem to be young children, too. I can look up, there's a hole in the tepee, you can see the stars.*

Janet: *Can you tell me who lives with you in this place.*

Heather: *There's a girl who's a little bit older than I. I think she's my sister. She seems to have a young little one with her, too, old enough to walk, she walks. There are two men over on the left side; they seem very serious, though. The laughter doesn't seem to be there now.*

Janet: *Can you tell me who these two men are to you?*

Heather: *They're older. I don't think my father's there. I don't have a father now. They're not brothers. But they have wisdom that I don't.*

Janet: *Can you tell me more of what they are talking about.*

Heather: *They don't seem to want me here, I don't know...I'm kind of curling up in some kind of fur...like a bear, I don't know. I feel like I'm covering up a little, kind of curled up in a corner. I want to know, want to listen, but they don't want to share right now. (Moving in time.) It seems dark right now. I don't see anyone anywhere.*

I asked Heather to take time...eventually telling me what she perceived.

Heather: *There's someone again, watching something. I...they're always off to my—they're over here (Pointing.) but I don't know...that same feeling comes back to my heart, it's like you can't get enough breath...I don't seem to be afraid to go. Why would I be riding at night, though?*

Janet: *Can you tell me where you are going? Are there others riding with you, or do you ride alone?*

Heather: *I'm alone, and I'm going fast.*

Janet: *And where are you going?*

Heather: *I don't know, but I'm scared now! There are a lot of them behind me.*[9]

Janet: *Okay, feel yourself riding as fast as you can, and tell me what's happening. Who is behind you?*

The emotion began to rise and Heather's heart pounded. She started to cry.

Heather: They're coming. There's too many of them, I can't go fast enough.
Janet: Who is it that's chasing you?
Heather: They're soldiers; there's a lot of them. I'm trying to get away, I can't go fast enough.
Janet: Let the memory come.
Heather: Now there's more of us, They're riding ahead of me and it's dark, it's dark everywhere.
Janet: They're riding with you? Where are they?
Heather: They're all around me, but...but there's too many soldiers, they're all behind us and we're riding as fast as we can go but we can't get away from them.
Janet: Where are you headed? Can you go for help?
Heather: There's nobody ahead of us, we're just riding, there's nothing up there.
Janet: What can you do?

Heather was breathing deeply and rapidly.

Heather: I don't know where to go, I don't know what...I just feel like if I stay and just keep riding, maybe I can go ahead of them. They're behind me, and...(breathing rapidly) all I see is men on horses, they're...(calming down.)...I don't know what happened, though. Did we get away enough, some of us? ...I didn't see us all die yet....
Janet: And where are you now?
Heather: It seems we got up on a ridge, and maybe it was sunrise coming, and the sun's up. It's coming up okay, and the light, they...they stopped...they stopped and they went back...we didn't fight them, though. They...we were just going away from them. We had to get away. I'm up on a hill. There's a few of us, but we're okay. There were just...there were a lot of soldiers, they were behind us.
Janet: What will you do now? What will you do next?
Heather: We have to go back to the village and make sure we're ready to go. We've gotta go. We've gotta move, 'cause they're gonna come back now, but they wanted to get us at

night, they wanted to see what we were doing. We were watching them, and then they saw us and they came after us. But they weren't ready, either. They went fast. There must have been only a few of us on horses and they...I don't know why, they seemed to have turned around, and they...but we know they're coming back.

Janet: *Allow time to pass, and allow your mind to move to the next important event that is affecting you now.*

Heather: *We're all riding in and we're yelling, screaming at them, "Come on, we've gotta go! Get packing, we've gotta get the babies!" The women are crying. They're scared, they don't know what to do. My friend looks at me and said, "Now it's time, you have to...no more dreams, you have to go, you have to do it now. You've got to fight, you can't watch the sun and say goodbye...."*

Heather's emotions rose and I encouraged her to let the feelings come. The tears flowed with her words of sadness and fear.

Heather: *...I don't want to...I'm too young. I don't think I should be...I'm not ready, I don't feel ready.*

Janet: *How do you feel?*

Heather: *Scared, but I've got to do it...they're not going to do it, they're not going to take my people, my friends. There are so many of them, there were so many behind me.*

Janet: *Can you fight them? What will happen to you?*

Heather: *I don't seem to have enough protection. I seem to be in the village, seems to be a lot of chaos. I don't know what to do, I'm trying to find somebody. I'm on my horse still, though.*

Janet: *Who is it you're trying to find?*

Heather: *Somebody I've to get, I've got to make sure they're okay. It's the girl...the girl who is my sister or my friend, I don't know who she is now. But she has that little one with her again, that...she's crying and I'm crying...(Raising her voice louder.)...I'm not going to see her again.... (Sobbing.) How can she protect...she can't...she's little...but we don't have a parent, there's no one there...she doesn't know what to do, she can't protect the little one. I have to go, I have to go to protect her before they get there, I have to go with the men.... (Sobbing hard.) I can't cry about it, I have to go...I can't watch the sunset any more! What can she do? I have to go, we have to go and fight them and we can't let them get there first. It hurts a lot!*

Janet: *I know, I know.*

Heather: *She just doesn't know what to do, there's stuff around her, people everywhere, she's just holding onto the baby and crying.... I can't help her.... (Sobbing.) ...I have to go, but I... They're calling me, I have to go with them, I don't want to leave her...there's no one to help her. All of the men have to go first, they've got to go and fight. There's dust everywhere, there's so much stuff going on. I keep looking back at her.... I don't really see much around her, she's just standing holding that baby, but there's so much dust around, it's like white everywhere, and I'm looking at her and she knows...she knows that I don't want to go. But if I can get in front, maybe I can do it, maybe I can protect her. I'm behind all the men, though. I don't want to see her die. I know I'm not going to see her again. I hesitate....*

I moved Heather further in time and asked what was happening.

Heather: *We left the village. They're out there, though. I see... they're blue.... I can see them...blue coats, I see it. They already got some of the other ones—they were ahead of us. We're too late, it's too late. They came behind us, they came behind us in the village when we left, we thought we were ahead of them. I don't want to see it, I don't want to see her screaming, I don't want to see it! (Speaking louder and overcome with grief.) I can't do anything! They're all around and there's nowhere to go. There's too many of them and there's fire...I can't look back anymore, I can't look back, I don't want to see her die.... There's screaming, seems to be open, a lot of field, but there's blue, a lot of blue coats all around us.*

I think she's gone. There's no noise now, there's nothing, there's just fire....

I moved Heather into higher realms of consciousness and asked the effects of that life upon her now.

Heather: The heart that hurts so much...something deeper. It's
always inside, and I haven't found it. It's an understanding,
doesn't have to be spoken.

I continued to question her about the current effects of that
earlier life.

Heather: Where am I going so fast? ...I'm angry, and I hate someone. I don't know if it's a someone or...I know better than
that, I know better....

I encouraged her to allow herself to feel the anger.

Heather: There's something in this hand.

Heather had suddenly dropped back into the lifetime memories
again.

Janet: What is it?
Heather: It's a knife, and it's got feathers on it. I can feel it going
into someone. I can...oh, I hate them! I see myself off the
horse. I seem to be trying to get up a hill, but I can't. The
pebbles, the rocks keep slipping from under my feet. They're
still coming by me, trying to get up there. I can't hold on
with my hands, the rocks keep slipping. They're only two or
three of them. They have hats on. They've got my ankle
and I'm struggling with them, and I don't want to watch....
Janet: Just let yourself see.
Heather: They couldn't have really done that, they couldn't.
Janet: Say the words and let's move on, say the words.
Heather: They have both of my ankles and I'm tied...ankles tied
down and they have hold of my arms and there's a sword
in the ground.... They keep putting it right down to my
back, but not on it enough to go into it, they're just cutting
it...just holding me over it. I can't get away from them,
there are four of them. They've got my arms and both my
legs. They're laughing. I can't get away from them. It's right
in my back, it's going.... They're having fun.

> *I don't know what they did. They were teasing me, that they were going to drop me right on it, but I don't think they did. But maybe they did and I didn't die yet, I don't know. I'm on the ground and they have my legs pegged and my arms pegged down in a big X. They're all around, screaming and hollering, but I don't know what they're going to do. I'm just tied down.*

Heather described how she was trying to get one ankle loose as I watched her right foot moving to try to release her ankle.

Heather: *But if I get loose, what would I do, where would I go? I see other ones of my tribe tied. There must be fire behind them so that I could see. There's light behind them so really it's just a silhouette of them. They're tied between two trees and their arms around. They've been tortured. They're not dead, they're just beaten. I see the one man who was in my tepee with me. He's older than I. His head is just hanging down, just...they've just beat him so bad. He doesn't have any spirit in him anymore. (Whispering.) So sad...he was one of the strongest ones...there's tears on his face.... He's just beaten....*

    It seems to be getting darker. My one ankle's loose but I can't get out of the...they're all around, still, they've killed everyone, everybody...there's nothing.... There's fire on down the hill.... I keep hearing them laugh, though....

Janet: *How do you feel?*

Heather: *Helpless. I'm ready to die.... I don't know what else to do.... I see the strongest one down, and he taught me.*

I moved Heather in time and she spoke very slowly and softly.

Heather: *It's dark out, I hear rain. I'm all wet. I'm tied behind my back and they're making me walk, pushing me. It's raining. There are a few of us, prisoners. They're making us walk... can barely walk. I hear a baby crying. They've got a rope around my neck...pulling on my neck...I'm walking behind a wagon, they're pushing us...trying to get off this hill.... He's pulling on it. He looked back at me and pulled it tighter around my neck....*

Janet: *How do you feel?*
Heather: *I just want to kill him. I can't stand it...but I can't do*
             anything.... It seems now that they've tied me to the wagon,
             actually tied the piece around my neck to the wagon...and
             we're walking behind the wagon. I'm floating right out of
             it totally.... I'm getting right out of it.

I directed Heather to look back at her body and tell me what she saw.

Heather: *They let the wagon go...just lying there on the ground with*
             a noose around my neck. There were two others...three be-
             hind the wagon....

I asked Heather to be aware of her thoughts as she left the body.

Heather: *I don't feel like I'm done, I don't feel finished. I didn't kill*
             enough of them...it's like revenge.... (Whispering.) ...I can
             see the sun...the golden fields...it's okay. I just saw her
             face...it's okay, she's smiling now.

The morning after Heather's regression she phoned. "How are you?" I asked.

"I don't think I've ever cried as hard as I did during that regression," she said. "My eyes are so puffy."

"How do you feel inside?" I inquired, going deeper.

"Good," she responded, "real good."

"Yes, it helps a lot to release that stored emotion," I said.

"I've been wondering, though, if that was the same Indian lifetime that you all have talked about, or if it is a different one. Did the information fit the knowledge that you have?"

Heather did not automatically accept memories of this Indian lifetime that we had talked about, and this was good. Sometimes it seems possible that the unconscious mind holds more than one Indian incarnation and might confuse them. It is also possible that Indian names get confused. Heather's name had been given by Michael as Thunder Cloud, but that name didn't fit the young brave in her regression. Michael had also gotten the name Warrior Heart, and Heather felt it to be her name in that lifetime.

"My sense is that it's the same lifetime," I said. "The similarities were there; there was nothing that did not fit. And each person had his own experience related to how death occurred." I explained that confusion on names had happened in my own experience. Through Sara my name had been given first as White Mountain. Through Dot my name had been given as White Cloud. It wasn't until my own regression during the holiday period that I realized my name had been Falling Star. I appreciated Heather's questions. It was certainly possible that she had retrieved memories of a different Indian lifetime, though my instincts said that this was the Oglala tribe.

Weeks later when I transcribed the tape of Heather's regression and heard her words, "I hear a baby crying," I saw a picture of the soldiers taking the baby, Elaine, to a white family[10] while Heather was being dragged by the wagon.

Chapter XV

Footprints from Kate's Indian Lifetime

Even when people with whom we interact are not aware of relationships that they have had with us in other lifetimes, they often speak and act out of their former roles, and I found that Kate had just experienced such a re-enactment. She was disturbed over the attitude of a woman, Judy DeGuzman, whom she had recently met and whom she recognized as her mother in the Indian lifetime. Judy had challenged Kate about leaving the convent and leaning on Michael too much. "I don't have twenty years to help you!" she had concluded.

"Twenty years to help me?" Kate wondered. "I haven't asked you to help me at all."

When Kate told me what had taken place, I was fascinated at how the unconscious mind expresses what the conscious mind does not acknowledge. Judy did not believe in reincarnation, so she had no acceptance for herself that she had been Kate's mother. Yet in speaking to a woman nearly her age she had become frustrated, as though she were replaying her role in the Indian lifetime where she had died in childbirth and left her little girl, Kate in this lifetime, to grow up without a mother. "Grow up because I'm not going to be around to take care of you," she had implied to Kate.

In our group we have learned to look with a new eye at everything that comes to us. We find something of value and something to discover in every new situation, and when I arrived Kate was beginning to process her interaction with Judy and, pushed by

Judy's challenge, to look more deeply into herself. In order to give us time to scan her life and understand more clearly its dynamics, she took time off from work. We found that her history had been interwoven from many threads but was focused on her own integrity. This allowed her to move into life as a nun and out again without interruption of her strong commitment to finding what was real.

My first question to her was how she came to believe in reincarnation when the church didn't teach this. Kate had had many transpersonal experiences that left her open to the possibility of past life.

> *I struggled with it, and it wasn't until I was in my early 30's that I believed in the concept, until I intellectually and seriously thought about that concept. Even though I'd always been open to the spiritual, and had certain experiences at home, experiences that my mother related that she had in terms of somebody appearing to her at the foot of the bed and finding out the next morning that the person had died. And she knew it, saying, "Yes, I knew so-and-so died because I saw him last night."*
>
> *So with that part, the connection with the spirit world, there was no difficulty in my family. We never talked about past lives that I can recall. The time of connection for me was when I was an adult, the time of meeting Michael and talking about past lives. I remember struggling a little bit with the concept. That was probably because of my conditioning. But one day, while stuck in a snowstorm, I had such a strong connection that it was as if a light bulb went on inside of me and I said, "Oh my God, it's a possibility." And the connectedness stayed with me, even when I was doing my master's work at St. Michael's.*

She reported that she had always felt a connection with Indian life, even as a small child pretending to be an Indian riding a white horse, and she had always felt a connection with the earth. She felt no conflict between Catholicism and Native American teachings.

I always felt a connectedness with the earth as I grew up. There was that strong attraction to the sacred, to the sacredness in all things, and I just always felt—as I said, I spent a lot of time by myself, I'm sure a lot of time in my head—and I was continually making connections with the land, connections with the earth, connections with the world of spirits.

When I asked her how she decided to become a nun, she said she had felt a need to share spiritual values. Catholic devotion seemed to be characterized by sacredness and awe.

To think back, we're looking back 28 or 29 years now, I believe that I was looking for a group of people who I felt shared the same values that I had. I was very much caught up in the spiritual, in the sense that that was what was most important to me.... In high school I decided I wanted to become a sister. And that's what I was going to do with my life. I was going to be able to delve more deeply into relationship with Jesus and be surrounded by people who valued what I valued.

During high school her draw toward the spiritual life increased, and at eighteen she entered the convent. The silence and introversion of the religious life were deeply compatible, and in such an atmosphere she grew inwardly.

The strong connection she had felt to the North American Indians since childhood prompted her to move on after eight years of administrative experience within the Catholic church. She began writing to Indian reservations. A friend sent her a little money every week so she could fly to a reservation and see for herself what it was like. Her first visit was to the Navajo and Hopi reservation near Ganado.

I spent about a month with my friend, did a lot of traveling, and spent a lot of time on the Hopi reservation, which is in the center of the Navajo reservation. Geographically it's right in the center, much much smaller land, space. I felt a deep affiliation with the Hopi because of their spirituality, tremendous spirituality.

Following this, she applied for a teaching position on a Sioux Indian reservation in North Dakota, and when she visited there she had a sense of coming home.

It was a little different feeling from the Navajo reservation, although I felt a similar sense of coming home. This time I knew I had been there before! That was the sense that I had.

I went for the interview and liked what the priest had to say. It was a fourth grade teaching position. I met with the administrator and talked with her and felt confident that this was the place for me. I loved the trees they had planted a long time ago, a lot of cottonwood trees that were natural to the area. The foliage touched something within me, along with the presence of the land in a spiritual sense. So not long after, I got the call about my acceptance and made the decision that yes, this was the place for me. I knew this was the place I was meant to be.

During her stay with the Sioux administrators she attended a Sioux Indian conference in North Dakota.

The conference was invaluable for me because of touching elbows, being in the same room with Native American people. I remember watching a woman in a calico dress, watching the lines in her face, the depth there. It's hard to explain, seeing the depth in the woman and a connectedness. She knew who she was, and with so many people that I had been exposed to in community and my life thus far I just didn't have that sense—it was like here is a holy woman. I was watching all those faces. You could see the trials in those faces, the suffering that they had been through. Not realizing my deeper connectedness at that time, I merged in my own way. There was such an intrigue and such a compassion that I could feel with these people, that I didn't realize that I had a deeper connection—but I could feel with them—feel at home with the group. I very seldom felt my whiteness, so to speak, unless someone else brought it out.

As Kate recounted this experience, her memories touched her heart and she was overwhelmed with emotion and tears. This deep emotional connection continued throughout the conference.

I began to cry...felt rather foolish at first because I was sitting with a lot of people on a small wooden bleacher and sobbing and trying to hold back the tears, sobbing and sobbing, whenever I heard—it was like the drum was my heartbeat and the heartbeat of a people, not only Native American people, but there was that connection, like the heartbeat of the land....

Now, that's the major pow wow that I went to in three years, and the drums tore at my heart. I just—I had no control. I would just sit and sob whenever I heard the drums and the singing—it was the drum beat and it was the Lakota singing.

Kate said she felt the presence of the land there in a spiritual sense and knew this was where she was supposed to be. Her religious community at home backed her decision.

During the time she taught at the Standing Rock Sioux Reservation she had a profound spiritual experience with her new friends when she was invited to pray in a sweat lodge with them, which was an honor.

I got to be close friends with a Native American man, Jody, and we had many conversations about spirituality and also talked about a sense of knowing one another. He was the first one that I found myself verbalizing to—that I had been on this land before, on this reservation—it wasn't called that—I'm not saying that particular spot, but I had been there on the prairie.

He accepted that very freely; he was a deeply spiritual man. He was the one who invited me to the sweat lodge. I had been invited more than once and kept putting it off. That was my own fear basically, my fear of enclosed places.

Kate described the ceremony of purification, formerly limited to men but now newly opened to women. She was hesitant to accept the invitation at first because she realized it was physically demanding, but when she was assured that even men felt the intensity of the heat, she knew she would do it.

> *There may have been a deeper fear that I haven't gotten in touch with but that was more on the surface of why I didn't do it right away. But I finally decided that I had to do this. And I don't know if it was in conjunction with an inner realization of my leaving there soon. I knew I didn't want to go without having experienced that. I would never have forgiven myself for not having done something that I wanted to do. So no matter what it cost me, I was going to do it.*

She had read about the ceremony and knew that coals were heated for hours, then taken within the dome where the ceremony was to be held.

> *So the evening came. I had read up on it, so I knew about the spirituality, the structure of the dome, the door facing east, and a path going from the door leading out a few hundred feet away where there was a huge pit where that whole day the rock gatherer would have been burning the rocks so that they were red hot when it came time for the ceremony. They were brought in and placed in the center of the sweat lodge. We sat cross-legged, touching knees, and you almost had to lean over because of the back of the dome.*

After all participants were seated cross-legged in a circle, water was poured on the coals with a ladle by a water bearer, and this released continuous hot steam. The ceremony is a cleansing one due to the intense heat. Often participants take in only a towel, but in deference to the two female participants, the garb that day was shorts and a shirt.

> *The flap was closed, and it was like being in the womb again and a birthing process. Joe started with a Lakota prayer, and I found no difficulty joining in. I knew a number of Lakota words; I listened for a while and kind of started singing along with them. Whatever it was, it seemed to come naturally. I just knew it was connecting with Great Spirit. And then he did some praying in Lakota and some praying in English for those who did not know Lakota.*

Kate constantly worried about whether she could manage the heat, but she was able to do this. During the ceremony a peace pipe was passed around and prayers were chanted.

> *One of the men began to pray for the group at this point. He spoke to the fish people and the various animals—the elk people, that one stands out in my mind. He gave personification to all these people, the tree people, sky people. He used the term "people" with them, and I felt it to be so right. He called upon the good spirits to be with us and prayed that no other spirit would enter in that would cause any rift or negativity in the group. He also prayed for spirit cleansing.*

After this each person offered up individual prayers and following this there was a brief respite outside the tent. There were four sessions, each more intense.

> *After each of the eight people prayed, we said again, "Mitakuye Oyasin," which means we are all related. That indicated we were finished. We did this four times. We went out of the lodge and came back in again four times. It got more intense. After each of the prayer times, they would open the flap, and it always felt so good when that flap was opened.*

The ceremony lasted approximately three hours with prayers and intense union with one another. Kate could see sparks of white lights and her friend said to her, "The spirits are here. All is good." Kate had no difficulty accepting the world of spirits.

During the last session the heat was even more intense,

If anyone came into it a little light-hearted in terms of prayer, by the time they got into the forth session of individual prayer they were so loosened up that everything just flowed out rapidly, whatever the inner cleansing was for. I remember praying for individuals, the family, for people everywhere, and my own inner healing. I was changed after that. The sweat just pours off, and I'm not one who perspires a lot.

Kate thought of getting out, but a participant assured her that the ceremony was nearly over and this enabled her to wait it out.

I realized as time went on the depth of that inner healing. After that sweat lodge I felt I could do anything; I no longer had a fear of that kind of enclosure. That fear went completely. So I knew I was home...I didn't have my regression until a couple of years later. I guess it was all an opening, to open to those avenues within me that would be receptive to something that I was receptive to and knew but had a fear of, the unknown.

In trying to evaluate the common ground between such teachings and those of the Catholic church, she felt there could be a connection between the seven sacraments of the Catholics and the seven sacred rites of the North American Indians. She was disturbed however, when the missionaries treated the Indians as pagans, even though the Indians had known God long before the missionaries arrived.

Kate gradually realized that she wanted a broader notion of God. In her perception the limited vision of the Church took people away from a true perception of God.

The clergy, I feel, connected the church with their concept of God and it was too small for me, much too small, much too limited, their notion of God. And so I began to have tremendous struggles with that. I had my own inner beliefs and there were a few people I would connect with here and there with whom I could talk about this, though there were never very many. Some of my innermost thoughts I could never expose to anybody until I met you and the group of people that I've been sharing with in the tribe.

It was this growing awareness that led Kate finally to break her ties with the Catholic Church and courageously to set out on her own road. Meanwhile, her years of teaching on the Sioux reservation had gradually drawn her into a bonding with the American Indian culture. Her lifelong fascination with Native Americans and her feelings of kinship with their rituals, especially with the sweat lodge ceremony, had been like footprints leading her back to her memory of her life in the tribe.

Chapter XVI

Channeling the Karma of the Tribe

Michael had taken some vacation days from work. We lingered over coffee and muffins on the patio, as we discussed some minor discrepancies in the information that had come through different people. My own name in the Indian lifetime had been one such example. Marda's was another. "Names are hard to get," Michael said, "and I'm not even sure it matters, except that in our own humanness we want to know. It was Roz who got the name Running Deer and I knew at that moment that it was my name in that life. Well, I suppose that a person could use their rational mind to say, "He has collected deer since he was a child," or "He has pictures and collectibles of deer around him," so the name Running Deer came to Roz."

I laughed at how we try to find logical explanations for the unexplainable as I pictured the elephants that Roz collected and commented, "But no one gave Roz the name of Little Elephant."

I Channel the Tribe's Karma

During this time in Naples, Michael gently pushed me to open up more, and I pushed him, also. I agreed to channel, but only if he would give me feedback afterward on what he sensed to be clear and accurate and what he sensed to be clouded or inaccurate. With that assurance I agreed, thinking that perhaps more information would come related to the Oglala incarnation. I relaxed and put myself into an altered state to allow information to come through. Then Michael posed a question that surprised me: "There has been talk of the karma of the tribe. I think there needs to be more understanding of that karma to further gain the ability to let it go." My channeled answer went on and on:

The Akasha[11] is that of experience and lives, of soul-movement, of body incarnations, and even thought and intent that resides for all time. The one who can tap into the Akasha is simply one who can tap into knowledge, wisdom, reach the vibrational memory and bring it in. Those vibrations can be picked up in many ways. They can be picked up as seeing-vision. They can be picked up as audio communication. They can be picked up as feeling-knowing. And always, it needs to be said, the interpretation is made by the person. Therefore, as she (meaning myself) fears interpretation because she knows the change in the physical dimension that brings interpretation, she avoids looking for herself. We appreciate the question.

There is karma that one soul brings into incarnation, the karma that comes from the cause and effect of energy from life experience, and the energy bringing into the birth, therefore referred to as karma, to move through that energy of blockage to free energy. One is born into a family, and there exists in the family relationship, karma—this word can be used. One is born into a race and therefore there is a color-race karma that exists with the individual based upon the race s/he has chosen. And therefore expanding out, there is a nation-karma that is taken on by living in a country, in this case the United States, in this time.

Truth is expanded as more is learned. The truth that now needs to go out in movement to those who would read and hear and "feel" this story, is one of the truth of the love of a people. These people are souls of a nature of connectedness to their divine self, individually, gathered together, expanded, as it was before, so it was in this tribe. The expansion of spiritual energy brought a greater growth of abilities, building into the soul this ability to love. A part of what the souls brought in was the ability to love and to be that love in a time in which a vibrational change was taking place to separate from the spirit. Let us explain the movement of the soul. Picture if you will, the yin-yang symbol. In the movement of the soul, what might be interpreted as good and bad, dark and light, is simply movement of the soul.

The souls brought in experience of connection to spirit and love. In the movement of soul-energy on a planet there was a move to more darkness from spirit, as seen (interpreted), more separation and movement to more separation from that God-energy. These souls needed to have their own experience in that time and in this time and space to return to contribute their memories, their experiences and their love and their power to speak out. In a world that does not believe a connection to the experience of soul memory, in a world that is searching and not finding that God-Source, in a world that has become intellect and does not trust feelings, in a world that has damaged the environment to almost no return, these people come. They come with their memories and with the courage to speak to a world that will perhaps not attack in that way, and yet there is fear on the part of some more than others. This group comes, to speak and to say, "This is my soul memory. This is my heart-felt experience. This is my spirit that speaks. This is my expression of love."

Each person makes his/her decision with his own spirit needs at this time, and it is all good and right. Karma? Karma of a tribe? It is all, as I have said, the time, the space, the race, the individual. Some chose to go to a cave. Some chose to try to consider negotiation. Some chose to fight, no matter what. It is all right and proper and good in the movement of the soul back to that Source of Oneness, and it is that Oneness that the deepest of us does remember and seek in Love and in Light.

Michael Channels

The information that came through during this session felt so general that I asked Michael to move into an altered state and see what further insights he could provide. Besides, I prefer to double check such material, just as I usually did with any psychic perceptions.

Michael relaxed himself and gradually moved into an altered state.

Janet: *Can you tell me what I looked like in that Indian life?*
Michael: *At what point?*
Janet: *About age 12 or 13.*
Michael: *I keep going to your moccasins, your moccasins and your buckskin dress. You seem to wear bracelets. You seem to be into ornate more so than a lot of the others, and I go to the scene where I saw you and Silver Eagle and I would come and join you. You would walk on his left and I would walk on his right side.*
Janet: *Yes, I've seen us walking that way. What do you see about my hair, face, anything around my neck?*
Michael: *Again, I see jewelry, bracelets, and even the clothing, you tended to be ornate with beads. You liked that.*
Janet: *That makes sense.*
Michael: *I see Silver Eagle reach up to a low branch on a tree and show us how the growth comes out in the buds, the tenderness of growth.*
Janet: *What age do you see him?*
Michael: *I'm surprised at his youth. I expected him to be much older, but he wasn't older. A mature man, probably in his late 30's to 40. At this point I see you and me about 13 to 15. You're not quite as old as I. The peaceful time...it became difficult for the talks and the sharing as we got older because times had more turmoil. So the softer teachings took place in a better time...many of those walks you took by little brooks that ran to the river. I see a band on each arm of Silver Eagle.*
Janet: *Do you know what they represent?*
Michael: *I don't know if it's something of his position, but they have like (indicating with his hand an inverted zig-zag design)*

> *going around the band, a bead design. I know occasionally*
> *he wore a buckskin shirt-type thing, but very often he*
> *didn't, and he wore his necklace.*

Janet: *Tell me about the necklace.*

The necklace in Mrs. D.'s painting fascinated me. I would have expected her to paint an Indian necklace of bone or teeth. Not so; it was quite unusual.

Michael: *It's hard because I already have impressions. I see small*
    green stones. I don't know why I keep getting a connection
    with Egypt. Maybe there was a connection with that life.

Janet: *Does the necklace have a connection to Egypt?*

Michael: *I think that it did. Another part of the necklace comes*
    down further and has a figure or design on it that is not of
    the Indian. It seems to represent a different spirituality than
    was lived in the Indian life. The Indian life lived fully in
    the earth plane taught spirituality fully through the earth
    plane. This necklace represents spirituality taught through
    higher learning; it doesn't fit with that place. It's subtle
    enough, it doesn't cause a conflict.

Janet: *How does he happen to have that?*

Michael: *It was given to him.*

Janet: *Do you know where it came from?*

Michael: *It was a gift from his father and the grandfathers; it has*
    been passed on.

Janet: *Okay.*

Michael: *It's been passed on.*

Janet: *Was there any conflict with me as a female becoming*
    chief?

Michael: *It wasn't seen as conflict because people were able to see*
    the soul, an evolved people. There was no threat; there was
    a balance of the masculine energy, so the feminine body
    was not a threat. The person housed there was recognized
    as who would hold that position, as Silver Eagle was. So
    you, too, would be....

Janet: *Was it automatically passed down to one in the family, or*
    not necessarily?

Michael: *Spiritual-family.*

Janet: *Okay.*

Michael: *It's an amazing concept that one would be sent of the same spiritual family...would follow the physical path. The vehicle would be provided through an acceptable manner. Extremely close-knit family spiritually, and that manifested that closeness in the physical.*

Janet: *You're speaking of the tribe as a whole, or my immediate family?*

Michael: *Your immediate family; it kind of radiates out. There's almost a denseness of closeness and it loosens as it goes out from that central place, it radiates out and that energy is felt and it keeps it close. But the further out from that you go, the looser it becomes. It's equally a part of...the closer to the center you get the denser it becomes.*

I then realized that Michael was talking about my immediate family in *this* life.

Michael: *There's a very strong connection or parallel between what was happening in the spiritual and in the physical. In this place, in many situations, there's a vast contradiction; there wasn't then. What was happening in one was paralleled or mirrored in the physical, as much as it could be.*

Janet: *Can you tell me whether my grandfather, Silver Cloud, was alive at the time I was born?*

My husband, Scott, had been my grandfather.

Michael: *I see him being in body when you were born.*

Janet: *I felt that.*

Michael: *The love is strong. You were a girl when he passed on, a young girl, but you did get to know him. The soul connection was so strong that there was not even a need for spoken words; that attunement brought knowledge. Again, a close, close connection with the spiritual. There was hardly even a veil. So when he passed over, he freely moved into the position of the grandfathers and that information continued to come through. It was a pleasant movement.*

Janet: *In the space where you are now, can you tell me if my name was changed, or whether the name given to me was my soul name?*

Michael:	*I see, feel, you being known by your soul name that was recognized very easily, freely, by your grandfather and your father. Your father saw you in the night sky—quite a sight! He knew...he recognized his daughter.*
Janet:	*Did I go through any kind of initiation period? Had I reached the point where I had gone through a vision quest or initiation?*
Michael:	*It was to come...so much was to come. I don't see the time of ritual...had never been allowed, it didn't eventuate.*
Janet:	*That was my sense also.*
Michael:	*You were still in the process of absorbing...so no, I don't see that that came.*

Michael had not met met my son Dan and knew very little about him. Not everyone has the need to check and double-check as I do. Nevertheless, confirmation helps ease my mind as I grasp with putting pieces together.

Janet:	*Can you tell me anything about Dan Cunningham?*
Michael:	*I see him. The ability was as with these people because of their connectedness with the spiritual realm to see and recognize the soul. He had sensitive gifts...has...that was recognized and he was encouraged to develop those. Though I'm fighting a title, I guess it would be considered...his movement was toward a medicine person, a seer, a healer. He has a sense of humor, often a clown.*
Janet:	*At what age are you seeing him? He is male?*
Michael:	*Yes, I'm confused on the age. I don't see him as a child.*
Janet:	*Okay, his gifts, then, go more toward a healer than a warrior?*
Michael:	*Yes—there's a sense of his soul in there...it would be a shame to waste them, and that was never done. Gifts were never wasted. They were encouraged to be developed. The one with a warrior heart was encouraged to be the warrior. The healer was encouraged to be the healer.*
Janet:	*Do you get a name?*
Michael:	*(Questioning himself.) One of flight???*[12]
Janet:	*Okay.*
Michael:	*...though I saw feathers; they seem significant.*

Since Michael had asked about the karma of the tribe, I wanted to see what insight he could bring while in trance state.

Janet: *In the place where you are, do you see an overall karma of the tribe?*

Michael: *The universe is energy; we are energy. Part of the evolution in energy is an understanding of its nature, of its movement. Each life holds an aspect of that movement toward the understanding. It is about the movement of energy; the evolution of it that we did not fully understand; we still do not fully understand. So we live it...living it on every level brings an understanding of it. Not only in thought or concept but in being one learns to understand it. Once it is fully understood, one doesn't view it as pain or pleasure but as the same, a completeness, a wholeness. It is a process.*

Janet: *I'd just like to open it up to see whatever information comes that might be of value for me to know related to that lifetime.*

Michael: *It is so important that the basic understanding and way of life that we lived be brought forward at this time because of what is most lacking at this time. Specifics come through that appease our logical mind, as more of a concrete place for our mind to grasp onto, but just enough so that the information can come through. What we lived is needed today, the understanding, and that constant basic message of—we use the word so loosely and even empty at times—of Love. But the real message of that, when lived, is anything but empty. The message must be taught that it wasn't the specifics, it wasn't the ending, but that what was lived needs to be heard today. That's why you do this.*

The position you were to hold, you held even before you were put there or went there. You hold it today; it's who you are. More information will come in terms of specifics through others' regressions, more can come through yours. It would be good for you to see.

Janet: *Is there a particular time period that would be good for me to go to?*

Michael: *Go to a time, one of a place of physical maturity, to view things with greater understanding and witness some of the ceremony and basic life. The interaction of the people is important because it gives that message again. It tells of the love that we shared and lived. Laughter, the games, games played...how we loved to tease White Fawn and run and hide behind the tepees. It was good; the love was good. Teach that.*

Chapter XVII

Viewing My Death: February 16, 1991

I had learned about the incarnation of Silver Eagle's tribe five years earlier. Again and again I had seen clients and friends go through these memories. Now my turn had come. Michael took time from work and after a light breakfast we went to his room. I made myself comfortable with large cushions on the floor and rested my back against the bed. To my right was a wall of mirrors, and straight ahead of me sliding glass windows opened to a small balcony. The room was immaculate, beautifully decorated and filled with light.

Soon this room was filled with the soothing aroma of burning sage that Michael had lighted. I began to move myself into an altered state of consciousness. Speaking very slowly and softly:

Janet: *I'm in a process of moving back. I'm taking Silver Eagle's hand, myself being small, maybe three or four years old. (My voice takes on a sense of wonder.) I'm reaching up high to take his hand, and walking...and he is talking to me about the birds and trees and the grass and animals and...how to listen! ...to the song of the birds and the words and wisdom of the trees. How old they are. (My voice grows more child-like.) They're older than I am! They've been here a long time, and they've seen many things. They have many things that they can teach us. The world is such an exciting place!*

190

There are animals—little animals, and medium-sized animals and big animals. And the size...the size of the animals scares me—because the big ones are so much bigger than I am, and I'm afraid of them. But he's teaching me that... "the size does not contribute to the strength or the power." The size...the size has nothing to do with the strength and the power. There is great power in the little ones—like me!

There is teaching that little ones give to the big ones. He makes me feel very good and very special because...it makes me not afraid to speak...because the big ones listen to me! So I look at the little animals, the rocks, insects...and they're doing their work. And they're building their homes. And they are helping each other.

And he takes me for walks by the river. I put my feet into the water...cold! And he tells me and shows me how the water moves...constantly moving...flowing, and sometimes it has waves in it. Sometimes it's calm. Sometimes a person has waves inside of them. Sometimes it's calm. And we need to respect the river...it teaches us so many things. It helps to clean...our clothes, it gives water to drink. It's always there for the horses and other animals. And we need to value it, give thanks for it...and the rivers inside of us need to be valued. We need to give thanks for the rivers inside of us, the waves and the calm. The water cleanses us, sustains us, and there is a wearing down of the hardness...that the water does. The river's rocks are smooth because of the constant movement over—long time.

Inside of us, the waters smooth the hardness. Make us...smoother! Nicer to touch.

Michael: *Is your father nice to touch?*

I felt a big smile come on my face that I recognized as Janet's face in trance and the child's face at the same time.

Janet: *Oh yes! He is. He feels good. He flows like the river. He listens to everything around him. He hears what the animals tell him.*

Michael: *Why does he tell you these things?*

Janet:	*He says that I'm important! And some day...he'll teach me...after I've learned about the animals, and the trees, and the river...then he's going to teach me more! He's going to teach me to be able to hear what the moon says...and he's going to teach me to listen...to what the storm speaks...and he's going to teach me to listen to the changes the moon brings...and...when I'm bigger...I'll learn more. I'll learn about the sun...and if I can be real good in listening...and I can hear, and see....*
Michael:	*Do you learn these things?*
Janet:	*I'm real good at learning! I...I learn, and I ask questions, and I don't understand so I ask more questions, and the answers that I get...I ask more questions...and when he's not around me, I ask other people questions because I don't know it all. I can't hear what the grass says.*
	Once I got down on my knees and put my ear down and I tried to listen real hard and I couldn't tell what the grass said. So I needed to find out how people heard what the grass said...and so I went around asking everybody.
Michael:	*Whom did you ask?*
Janet:	*I go to...I sometimes go to the medicine woman and the medicine man, and I ask questions...I sometimes ask my friends, and I ask the hunters and the women. Everyone says things in different ways. Then I tell my father about what I've learned...and he asks me to tell what the people have said.*
Michael:	*What does he say?*
Janet:	*He smiles at me and he picks me up. He likes our walks. He tells me I'm special. Everybody loves him. He talks to people and he listens...and people listen to what he says... because he has... (emotion rose in me and I took a deep breath.) ...he has something Great Spirit gave him!*
Michael:	*Can you take me to a time when you're older?*

After a few moments of silence my voice took on a tone slightly older.

Janet:	*I have friends. We ride together and we play games. And we work. My father teaches me to be strong. I have some tasks to perform that the others do not have. We have*

much work to do and it is good work as each person is a part of our whole family and every task is important. Every task is depended upon for the creation of a harmonious family. And if there is difficulty, harmony must be brought into the difficulty so that the work is smooth and can be counted upon by others. So each person has his responsibilities and his talents that can be depended upon. Much of my teaching has changed from listening outside of myself to training inside of myself. I am taught to concentrate my thinking and to concentrate my hearing and I am taught to hear inside what another person is feeling. I practice hearing inside what someone outside of me is thinking and feeling.

Michael: *Why do you do these things?*

Janet: *It has been said by the grandfathers that I walk in my father's shoes. He is very wise...and so he teaches me...so that I can walk in his shoes and have the ability to listen to other people's hearts and help them to do their tasks in happiness. When people work in happiness, their work is good. When they are not happy in their hearts with their work, their tasks, their work is not good. Their peace is not good, and the others around them are affected by their not-good-peace. So it is very important to listen to the heart...to have good work, and peace for our people.*

Michael: *How do you feel about walking in your father's shoes?*

Janet: *I cannot do it!*

Michael: *It is said.*

Janet: *The grandfathers have said I will walk in my father's shoes. My heart...I am not ready.*

Michael: *Can you take me further?*

Janet: *I have learned to not cry out in pain sometimes when pain is there. I have learned to not cry sometimes when tears are there. I have learned to be strong and to walk tall. I have learned to speak with an understanding. They say that I have a wisdom that exceeds my years...that I'm little but not little, that I am young but not young.*

Michael: *How old are you?*

Janet: *Many moons have passed since the time of my coming. I have a brother. He's going to be a warrior. He likes to fight in games; he often wins.*

Michael: *Can you describe him to me?*
Janet: *He has a strong action body, full of energy and movement.*
Michael: *He's younger than you?*
Janet: *Yes. He…while I sit and think, he rides and is beginning to learn the skill of the bow. He[13] is little and he's determined.*
Michael: *Tell me about your people and what is happening.*
Janet: *My father walks among the people, talks and listens to them. There is a hunt upcoming; it is needed. And there is preparation for the hunt. The warriors will go out and bring back food. The women will prepare the meat. We will have food to put away for our cold time. And there is an excitement in preparation for this time. My father walks…he's talking and listening. When there is a disagreement, he brings the people together to find a solution and agreement among themselves, and it is good.*
Michael: *Tell me about a disagreement.*

My mind started to move to a typical disagreement that may occur, then bypassed that and moved on to a bigger issue.

Janet: *There are things that I have not heard before, that people now speak of. I hear things of men who want to take our land. I hear words about them coming and there is fear in people's hearts. There is fear in the air. There is change in the wind.*
Michael: *Who are these people?*
Janet: *I hear words that speak of white faces; I have never seen white faces. There is a discomfort that I have never sensed before. It feels like something that I have no knowledge of. I listen to everyone's words and I listen to their hearts…and I hear screams that aren't around.*
Michael: *Of the white faces?*
Janet: *The winds bring the change with the white faces, and in the winds I hear the cries. I fear greatly with what I hear. I look around, and our tribe is safe and good, and we do our work, and our life is as it has always been…and yet nothing is the same as it was…because the rivers, the storms, and the trees and people's hearts and their words are filled with fear of these people. What is to become of us? Everyone looks to my father for the answers; everyone*

looks to my father for the wisdom of the chief. And I see that he has seen things that he wishes not to speak of; he has deep, deep pain in his heart. There is a heaviness in his walk, a sadness in his eyes.

Michael: *Is he sad at these white faces coming?*

Janet: *Yes. There are some of the warriors who have said, "We must fight; it's our land, we must fight for what is ours. We live with Great Spirit; we must fight, it cannot be taken away." There are others who say, "Let us move, let us run, let us go." There are those who want to strike first for greatest benefit in the fight. And there are those of vision who have said, "The land will be ours no more." The struggle to decide to fight or move my father takes into his heart. He has said, "Let us live in harmony with these people. Our land is great and gives to us; we give back. Let us live in harmony with these people; let us offer them peace so that we may live and watch our children grow." And yet as he speaks of harmony and I see what is in his heart...there is such pain as I have never seen before...or felt before. There is much confusion, much confusion. We are not in agreement. We are not in harmony. We are not in peace. There is much confusion. What will become of us? We cannot **not** live, we cannot **not** survive. We must stay. Are we to stay here; are we to move? We cannot allow ourselves to be destroyed. What do we do; how do we fight these people? Some have said that they come like waves over the mountains. They have seen in visions the waves over the mountains, they keep coming, they keep coming...how can this be?*

Michael: *What decision is made?*

Janet: *The decision has been made for us. These men do not want to live in harmony. These men...there have been attacks. (I took a deep breath.) Little Feather...was found.... I think Running Deer found her.... (I sensed Michael crying as he sat near me—I knew he was seeing the pictures.) Who are these people? These are not people that we can talk to. The animal kills for food...for survival...or purpose...and it is Great Spirit's way. This must be something less than Great Spirit's way. There is great sadness among our people. We are frightened. We*

don't know how to deal with...(Deep breath.)...such as
these. There have been a few who have chosen to go away.
They have left our tribe. They will not fight and have
already left. My father has asked, "Who will stay, who will
fight, who will go?" We will fight. We have no choice. We
have nowhere to go where the white faces will not be. There
are some warriors who are very strong, strong protectors of
our people. So we prepare.

The visions keep coming stronger. The visions tell of
the land belonging to white faces. (I took a deep
breath...and spoke slowly and very softly.) Have they been
taught...(Whispering.)...to listen to the grass? Do they hear
the trees? Have they learned...to hear the messages of the
wind? The land must be heard. (Deep breath.) The land
must be protected...and so we fight, to protect our people
and to protect the land. And the land speaks to us.

Michael: What are you doing?

Janet: We are doing our work. There is a sudden...(I paused for
a long time without talking.) ...The shock of movement
holds me in time.... There is a...there are horses...there is
yelling...there are guns...there are screams...there are arrows...there are swords...there is...there is fire. There is
running...there is blood. There is...this is something we
have never experienced....

Michael: Where are you?

Janet: I see tepees and fire.... I see people...being grabbed. I
see...I see my people...running...knives, arrows, the noise,
screams.

Michael: What do you do?

Janet: I stand frozen in horror of what I see. I cannot
move...I...surely this must be something I will wake from.
This cannot be real. I'm back aways at the edge of our
tepees. The men ride...I feel a vengeance and a hatred that
has never been felt in my being in all my sensing, in my
teaching, I have never experienced such in another. This is
beyond anything of control; this is beyond our capabilities.
We have no defenses to such a feeling as this. This is a
purposeful destruction. We are unable to combat such as
this. I'm taken away...someone...someone pulled me away.
We are running. I smell the fire, I hear the screams. We are

	running. I wonder where my friends are. I wonder what has happened. I wonder about my people...who is alive and who is dead. I don't know what has happened.
Michael:	*Where are you being taken?*
Janet:	*We're running into the woods, running away from the white faces, running to someplace of safety, running.... We seem not to be followed, their attention is to the village. The fires...I smell the smoke, I smell the fire. We gather the ones that we can. There are scouts who have gone out to find others who have survived. (Whispering.) So many of our people are gone.*
Michael:	*Where are you now?*
Janet:	*We are preparing...talking among our people, to see what to do next, to make decision about where to go. There is no winning. How do you fight hatred? How can a people fight hatred? Can waves and waves of hatred across the mountains be fought? Where is the answer? I cannot understand. Have we been abandoned by Great Spirit? What have we done? Where...where did we go wrong?*
Michael:	*What do you do next?*

I took a long time trying to perceive what was happening while at the same time my mind could not seem to look at it. This was a repeat of what had happened during the holidays. Would I be able to continue? I raised in consciousness and kept my eyes closed speaking to Michael more as "Janet."

Janet:	*There has been like an escape...like my mind moved out from that experience. What I'm seeing is light and energy, like I moved myself out of it...so I have to go with thoughts instead of what I was seeing or experiencing and see if that brings me back into the memory. I think that there were only a few warriors, women and children. So few members of the tribe that are left. Incredible grief, sorrow. My father had no idea how many warriors we lost; it was a sudden attack. We simply don't know what to do. There is such confusion, such sadness, such a sense of loss. (Deep sigh.)*
Michael:	*Where is your father?*

Janet: *He is away with some of the men. I've been trying to see*
               something and my mind is fighting the seeing of what
               happens next.

I took a long time in my mental battle and eventually dropped
into a deeper trance-state again and continued.

Janet: *There are men who come…there's fighting, fighting but not*
               killing. There is (Sigh.) …There is taking of the women in
               our gathering…there is threat of death and laughter and I
               don't…I can't find the words….

I realized that I was seeing the raping of my mother and the other
women.

Janet: *The men grab and throw down, and push, and hurt…(I*
               sensed my own rape but stayed separate from it.)…and
               take, and laugh…and destroy…the spirit. (Speaking softly
               with a determination.) I protect my spirit! The body can be
               taken…but I protect my spirit. I remove myself. I will not
               be in this place with these feelings!

Tears rolled down my face. Michael put tissues into my hands and
I heard him blow his nose.

Janet: *I will not stay…in the presence of such anger and such*
               hatred. (Crying, feeling the determination of Falling Star.)
               I will not allow my spirit…to be destroyed…in this way. I
               remove myself from my body.

The tears fell down my face and I wiped them with the sleeve of
the sweatshirt that I wore.

Janet: *I am not strong enough…in my body to fight…(Crying.)*
               …There are too many, they are too strong. I cannot…stay
               in my body and fight…. I know how to get out of my
               body…. They cannot get me there. When I'm out of my
               body…I'm safe.

A feeling of uncontrollable grief began to overcome me...and yet an internal strength was also present as I continued.

Janet: *I will not scream. I will not yell out in pain...they will not reach me. So, I don't feel what's going on in my body, I don't know, I don't know, I don't know what happens. But I do feel their anger, I do feel their hatred. (Continuing to speak with much pain.) ...and I do not understand why we are so hated. I do not understand what I have done. I feel weak. So much of my strength is gone.*

Michael: What are you seeing now?

Janet: *(Almost inaudible.) ...They have just found my father. (Deep breaths.) ...and they're dragging him...hands bound, dragging him.... He is so strong. (Gasp.) ...He is so strong. (Very slowly with great grief.) ...Where does his strength come from? I am so tired, and weak. (I took two very deep breaths and my voice rose slightly.) ...But if I'm going to walk in his moccasins... (Crying, I wiped my face with tissues and my sweatshirt.) ...I have to find it someplace! ...So...I look to him...(Crying outright.)...and he gives strength to me...and...(My conscious mind became aware of Michael crying.)...(Deep breaths.)*

Michael: What do you see?

Janet: *So I can do this...and I can go through this...and...I will make him proud of me....*

I sense myself moving my position from being slumped over to sitting a little straighter.

Janet: *So I bring that strength into my body...and into my mind... the way he taught me to do...and...my hands are tied. There have been others whose hands have been tied...and...it can't last forever.... I can...I can wait. I can be stronger...than their hate.... I just won't look at them...and I won't...I won't see.... I'll just...see...what I want to see. So I look at the sky...and I look at the leaves.... (Crying, and yet staying in control so that I won't fall apart.) ...and...when I get so scared...I look at my father...and I tell him in my mind...that they won't get to me. (Crying.) ...and he gives me his strength and...and so*

I don't see anything but the sky, the clouds, and the leaves...and my father's strength. And it can't last. I can wait. And...so I don't see them. And I won't look at their faces! (Determined.) I won't see anything but what my mind wants to see! I never look at their faces, and they get angry at me...'cause I won't look at them...I don't care...'cause I'm strong...(Sobbing.)...and I'll show them...I'm strong!

(Almost inaudible whisper.) I have to go.... I don't want to leave my father...alone...(Sobbing.) ...I can't stay...any longer.... He...he tells me to go...(Sobbing.) ...He's telling me to go.... I have to 'cause I can't stay any longer...but I don't want to leave him. I can't...I can't...but he's telling me to go.... He's telling me that if I go first, if I go first...then he'll come. I have to go first. I have to go first, he's telling me. I have to go...before he can leave... that he has to be the last...and I can't be the last one, he has to...so, he's telling me to go and he'll follow me. (Gasp, and several deep breaths.) (Several more deep breaths as I felt the release of passing into spirit.)

Where is he? Where is he? They're doing something.... They're doing something to my body.[14] They're doing something...and...he cannot bear...any...more...pain. He has taken on...the pain of every...one...of his people, every one of his people. And they're doing something...and, he cannot...bear...this pain any longer. (Sigh.) But I can't find him. He's not there, and he's not here. I don't...I don't know where he is. He told me he would follow me...and he told me to leave, and I can't find him. I...I need to find him.[15]

Michael:	*Where are you?*
Janet:	*I'm in a place where I can breathe. And there...there are lots of people around me....*
Michael:	*Can you see the Light?*
Janet:	*I...I know that it's here; I can't see it. I sense, I feel, I don't see...I feel confusion, and I feel hurt, I feel anger, and I feel horror, and I feel hatred and I feel love and I feel acceptance...and I feel all of these things, confusion, and...and we seem to be moving.... We seem to be moving*

> *to (sigh...) to more peace. I can't find him. I don't know*
> *where to look...but I have to find him.*
> Michael: (*Whispering.*) Go to the Light...you'll find him, go.*

It took a few minutes to pull myself back to the present reality. I had been in the regression for two hours. Michael and I wiped our faces and blew our noses. I put my arms around him and gave him a hug, saying, "You certainly have patience."

"God, I could never be a regression therapist," he said. "I wanted to get out of there so bad!"

"I know that it wasn't easy for you," I told him. "Thank you."

Michael and I had lunch and then went for a long walk on the beach. Feeling the sand beneath our feet, the warm afternoon sun, and the movement of our bodies walking helped to ground us in the present. We didn't sit—we kept walking. We turned the subject to current-life experiences, about love and relationships and the journey of the soul.

I felt less "present" that evening when Kate and Michael and I went out to dinner at a small Italian restaurant in Naples. We were seated at a private table against a mirrored wall, separated from people on the other side of the room. We ordered a bottle of wine and I slowly sipped my customary one glass, which would last throughout the evening with half being left.

From time to time I felt unable to follow the conversation and jokes that Kate and Michael tossed back and forth. Noting my lack of presence, they sensed that the regression had jolted my mind and energy system.

Suddenly Michael looked deeply into my eyes and with an unexpected force in his voice said, "The issue is not yours; you are carrying an issue from childhood. It's not yours to carry!"

What?! What did I miss? We had not been talking about me at all, let alone about my childhood. I stared at Michael. What was he talking about? "My childhood? What issue?" I asked.

"What? What issue? Your childhood?" he questioned back.

Had I jumped into the Twilight Zone? Michael seemed not to know what he had said. I continued to stare at him and repeated, "You said something about an issue from childhood."

"I did?" he asked with surprise. "I said what?"

Kate confirmed, "Yes, that's what he said. I heard it, too."

"Whoa, I don't like this," he said. "Janet, what happens when you are around?"

I again repeated his sentence and Michael had no recollection of having said it, but when I prompted him, "What is the issue from my childhood?" he gave in to channel the information and began to talk in a straightforward and forceful manner. I was glad that we were seated far from everyone else in the restaurant.

"You are carrying an issue from childhood. It is not yours to carry!" he said raising his voice.

"Are you talking about my mother? Am I carrying her issue?" I was trying to get the message and at the same time I wondered *who* was speaking to me through Michael. Michael had slipped into an altered state of consciousness with eyes open; he was very alert. I knew that someone was trying to get an important message to me.

I thought of how important emotional and mental balance is to me...and had a flash of so many fears that I had grown up with. What was I being told? He went on strongly: "It is not yours to carry—you have the balance. You absorbed in your childhood; it is not your issue!"

I stared into Michael's eyes while he continued the message. Kate recognized what was happening and began to enjoy it thoroughly. Knowing Michael's hesitation to trust himself in such matters, I was thrown off guard at what had begun to take place. I knew I wasn't grasping every word the way I usually did.

Soon, the message having been given, Michael settled into his own personality and we discussed what had just occurred. Aside from the initial sentence Michael's experience had been similar to mine—a feeling of standing back internally and observing himself give information that poured forth.

After this odd experience we both realized that we had to explore the issue still further. I had done the long-feared regression, but the day before my flight home Michael and I decided to see if more of Silver Eagle's teachings could come through. We again settled comfortably in his room and I began to put myself into an altered state. For some reason, I had difficulty "getting there," and Michael sensed it. He opted to try to "lift" me in consciousness. With no words spoken between us I felt him move to a deeper state than I had reached; at that point I felt grounded and "reality based."

Well, if he is the one going into trance instead of me, we might as well work with this, I thought, and began to ask Michael what he was seeing. He started talking, and suddenly realized what was taking place. "Hey, this isn't supposed to be happening," he said, and brought himself to a more conscious state where we both joined in laughter. "Now I know I couldn't be a regression therapist," he added. "I thought I could pull *you*, and instead I went out myself."

This was true. I felt mentally grounded, a necessity in my work, and that is exactly why I struggled so much with the "expanded realities" that had become so much a part of my life and work.

With the release of laughter we calmed down and I tried once again to relax my body and mind. This time the relaxation came naturally, and I moved to a time of teaching by Silver Eagle:

> *As I grow a little older, Silver Eagle continues to take me off alone daily, most of the time, to be taught. Sometimes my friends may walk alongside for a while. Sometimes they wander off or find something else to do. But for me there is nothing that is more interesting or more exciting or more…there's nothing that draws my attention more than what my father is teaching me. I am captivated by his wisdom and his knowledge and his understanding and his caring…and the qualities that he has that I would love to be able to copy, that I would love to be able to bring into me and live.*
>
> *There is a deep peace within his heart and a love that is so expansive, a caring about all things and all people. There is a light about him that is admired by his people. He is chief, not because of a name or title of chief…but he is chief because of who he is. He is chief because of…the light and the strength of his spirit.*
>
> *He teaches me about Great Spirit, and he teaches me about my spirit, and he teaches me most in what he lives. His words help me to understand and to comprehend, his words help me to analyze, to communicate for more knowledge, and yet I learn*

most about the spirit of this man in the way that he lives. Because he truly lives what he teaches.

The spirit of every person lives within their heart, and the spirit must be nurtured, supported, loved, and cared for...and must be freed. The spirit within each one of us comes into the body to express itself, and it is important that the chief contribute to helping the person express this spirit. So the chief must be able to see into the person, and the chief must be able to feel what the person feels. In doing so, the chief can contribute to the unfolding of the spirit. Those warriors of spirit must express their warrior nature and need the time to learn those skills, the place and opportunity to express that nature.

There are those whose spirit needs to express a mothering, caring for, nurturing side, and they must have the time and the space and the encouragement and support to express their spirit in that manner.

There are those whose spirit calls them to connect with healing properties of nature and the body, and they need to be given the time and the space and the opportunity to grow in that knowledge so that it may be expressed.

In all ways the encouragement and support of the chief is to express the spirit as one becomes more and more attuned with the spirit. In the process of becoming attuned to the spirit, one moves to the heart...to see moves the heart to feel, moves the heart to know.

I am being taught to see into the heart, and I am being taught to feel another's heart, and I am being taught to listen and hear what one's heart says. And if I can learn how to do this, I can help others in their spiritual quest. When one has found that spiritual quest for himself or herself, his life path is good and in harmony with his spirit. When work takes people in a direction that is not in harmony with the spirit, it causes a lack of harmony within. If this is not understood and a correct path found, that lack of harmony begins to eat away at the spirit. The unhappy spirit over time, then, is expressed in a person—is unhappy, angry, distressed, lacking in energy. The body begins to express the lack of harmony; the body expresses the unhappiness.

Sometimes the body hurts, becomes sick, brings to it accidents of nature. And when these things happen, we try to search within the spirit to find reasons why these things have occurred.

Our people are quite attuned to Great Spirit and the land. And this attunement moves us to a connection to our own spirit, and yet sometimes help is needed to find one's spirit. We are all connected. The animals, the plants, the water, the air, the sky, the rocks, the land...we are all connected. We support each other in harmony, and when there is a separation from the spirit, this separation causes disharmony. The human being can then cause disruption within the circle of life. How important it is for us to be in harmony with ourselves and then assist others. The circle, then, moves out to support and love the land and the animals and all that is.

It is, I am told, quite easy for some people to separate from their spirits, become not-in-tune with their inner being. And those people need more assistance in helping themselves to find—again—that connection to Great Spirit, because it is Great Spirit that feeds our inner spirit.

Great Spirit is in all things. Great Spirit is in the water, and the grass and the trees and the birds. Great Spirit resides in all places and in all things. In acknowledging Great Spirit's wisdom, we must acknowledge the wisdom that resides in the plants, acknowledge Great Spirit in the animals, acknowledge Great Spirit in the land, the rocks—it all teaches. We learn from the rocks when we value the rocks. We learn from the animals when we value the animals. It is this respect for Great Spirit within the tree that calls us to respect and honor the tree.

The human one has responsibility. With a greater knowledge, with a greater wisdom comes a greater responsibility. With the understanding and knowledge of Great Spirit's presence in all things comes the responsibility to honor Great Spirit in all things. If there is within a person a lack of that respect, a lack of that acknowledgment of Great Spirit, he can separate himself from Great Spirit's being in other creations and become a destructive one, destroying harmony, destroying the support of the circle of

*life, destroying a part of his spirit. For in the innerconnectedness,
we are as one.*

    *I understand what my father says, partly because he teaches
it, but more because he lives it. I see him listen to the other
creations and value and respect them. I see him honor all things.
I see him give love to the little shoots of new life plants. I see
him honor all things. Such a gentle, gentle soul that becomes
such a powerful, powerful man. It is as if the more he listens to
other creations, the wiser he becomes. It is as if the more he
gives of himself, the stronger he becomes. I watch and I study
and I see a lot. I am learning to feel what another feels in his
heart. I am learning to hear the voices in the winds, and I have
so much more to learn. I hope that Great Spirit will fill me more
and more. I do not feel that I could ever take my father's place.
I will not think about that now. For now, I will learn and keep
my connection to Great Spirit and learn to honor all life and all
creation. I understand that this is the only way to have the peace
and harmony that we desire and need. It is a good life and we
are trying to move to more peace and more love and more
harmony in our Being in our family.*

    *Time is needed. Aloneness is needed, and quiet is needed to
listen to Great Spirit inside you. We work hard and we
understand that the silence and the private time, the quiet time,
is a part of our work. When the body passes on, it is the spirit
that lives. And so it is the spirit that must be filled, the spirit that
must be nurtured; it is the spirit that must be loved. It is the
spirit that lives on. These are some of the teachings of my father.*

Following this session Michael and I took our last walk on the
beach. The warm afternoon sun felt good and we stayed for a
spectacular sunset. I talked with Michael about my hesitation in
writing some of the personal material about people in our tribe,
including those who gave me permission to use their names. And—I
knew four people who had been soldiers in that life.

Michael said, "Janet, you write this book for your own
healing...and the healing that it will bring to many, many people. It
is more important than any one person's ego. Write it as it actually

happened—don't leave anything out because of any one person. That would dilute the truth. We are all a part of this story; it is *our* story. Write it as you know it. You are the only one who can do that."

Chapter XVIII

Resolution: 1992

I said goodbye to my dear friend Kate and my "deer" friend Michael and flew back to upstate New York. The next day I collected my mail at the post office and went home to open it. The patent attorneys had sent my official Trademark Certificate of Registration for my business—Breakthroughs to the Unconscious® ...and for my logo, a drawing of my hands breaking the ropes that had held me back. I had begun the process of registering my logo nearly three years earlier and had wondered why it was taking so long. Yet only after *I made my own breakthroughs to my unconscious*—to the end of our tribe's massacre where I had broken the ropes that had held me back—did the universe respond.

I basked in my new-found strength for three days, touching base with Roz, DeLaine, and Marda. Scottie came to visit, and I spent the weekend with him and Scott in Elmira. My mind was filled with information; the regression had been invaluable to me and I felt ready to work on the book.

However, when I returned to my apartment in Owego I couldn't get into writing. I busied myself with transcribing tapes and assumed that the writing would come. I turned my attention to setting up seminars, moving out more with my work, but once again I felt fear rise. I grew utterly frustrated with myself.

Understanding the source of deep grief and fear in my unconscious had been a first step. It was now necessary to move beyond it. Again, I questioned myself, and I came to understand what was holding me back from finishing the book. The programming of my culture and society said this story was not possible, and I knew that I could not prove that the tribe existed. I hesitated to conclude a narrative that might not be acceptable.

But I knew that these memories resided in the unconscious minds of each of these people who had recovered the Indian lifetime, their pain, their anger and grief. I shared in the joy of remembering and reconnecting with this very special group of men and women. All of us were pulling out of discordant times in our lives and not only were becoming healed ourselves but were moving into a place where we could bring healing to others.

For instance, Marda's talents and personality had begun to blossom; she had been asked to serve on the faculty of a holistic health center in New England. For seven years Marda had wondered, "What am I doing in this group of people?" After the release of her powerful childhood and past-life memories, Marda's gifts began to open—she started to see other people's past lives. She looked happier and felt healthier than she had ever remembered being.

The healing energy encompassed not only our tribe who had been massacred but extended to the soldiers who had killed us. A former client and friend invited me to lunch. We met after he had gone to DeLaine for bodywork. During their session he mentioned the movie *Dances With Wolves* and DeLaine told him to watch it several more times because "more information will come." He told me that the first time he saw the movie he cried for hours afterward. When he asked a psychic about this strong reaction, he was told that it was because of an Indian past life. He knew that I was writing about an Indian life and asked me if I had completed the story.

I told him that it was about a group of people who had memories of being together. He asked the name of the tribe and where they were located. I replied that the tribe was Oglala in what is now the Dakotas and told him that there had been a total massacre of the tribe.

He interrupted me. "Janet," he said, "I have to tell you that I am getting a really uncomfortable feeling. Janet, I was there." As he squirmed in his seat I wondered if I should tell him my suspicions. I hesitated for a few moments, remembering the last time we had lunch about a year earlier. At that time, sitting across the table I looked at him and had a flash of realization—*he had been a soldier in that life.* Still, not willing to trust myself, I had filed it in my mind and told no one.

On this day I decided to be forthright and tell him what I had sensed. "Oh no!" he replied, as his own realization began to come. He reminded me of one of the past-life regressions we had done in which he saw himself as a soldier in a blue uniform. The regression involved a relationship issue and had not taken him to any interaction with Indians. Consciously I had forgotten that lifetime until he reminded me of it. *I did* remember another regression—to his birth in this life. This gentle and soft-spoken man had been furious, and spewed forth profanity as he angrily yelled about being born: "How do they expect me to *defend myself* with this little body!"

I assured him that there is no conflict between us now and that we are all on the path of healing, Native Americans and soldiers together. This man has worked with me for two years delving into his unconscious mind and has spent many more years in intensive self-healing, both mentally and emotionally. He has devoted his life to sharing his spiritual walk with others.

All of us who had been members of the tribe were experiencing various transformations in our lives. In the early days of our relationship, Joyce Smith had said, "This is a group of healers who have returned." At the time she said it we were not yet a group of healers, but since then I have watched as *first we healed ourselves and then began to change professions.* Today every person is active or moving toward some form of the healing arts or interest in healing Mother Earth. But in spite of the obvious movement in the group toward healing, I still was having difficulty writing.

I had seen—and it has already begun—that our small group would move out across the United States and into other countries to gently *live* a message of the Power of Love that transcends time. I went to my set of Runes[16] for insight into my unconscious, asking, "why, why now, am I so afraid?!" I pulled the Blank Rune:

The Massacre

Blank is the end, blank the beginning. This is the Rune of total trust and should be taken as exciting evidence of your most immediate contact with your own true destiny.[17]

In spite of this reassurance I processed again my awareness that my inner truth and all of my experiences with these many people over the years could not be proven, any more than one could "prove" in a court of law that he/she loves a spouse. *Inner feelings and inner knowing are not proven through objective, external measures.* I might be judged as illogical or naive by some, or even threatening by others. Once again, I could be "attacked and hurt" for just *being*.

Apparently this fear of being attacked was now the fear in my unconscious that I had to move beyond. I sat down at the computer and began to write the story. The writing finally poured out of me, poured so freely that I wondered, *When will the story stop?* Roz was concluding his paintings. DeLaine had just seen the painting finished earlier of White Fawn. "It is a tribute to you and all that you did for our tribe," Roz had told her.

He was now beginning the final painting of his four-panel series. I had been there to assist him by moving him into an altered state. I watched in amazement as he began to sketch on the large canvas with his eyes closed. He had completed his first two paintings in two and a half months, but the painting of the massacre proved to be a struggle every step of the way the way. It took eight and a half months to finish and was a graphic composite of his memories.

As I stared at this canvas I could see Silver Eagle's body after his death—arms and legs torn from their sockets. Roz had painted White Owl (Timothy) with an arrow in the chest, Flaming Arrow (Deb) hanging, Walks Tall (Scottie) on the ground with knife in one hand and hatchet in the other, and me, chest cavity ripped open, hands tied and hanging, facing Silver Eagle. It was over.

Roz had completed his version of our story, and now it was up to me to finish mine. There was still so much healing going on, however, that I rationalized that I should not conclude our story. Perhaps, I thought, I'll meet still others from the tribe or some of the soldiers who attacked us. Perhaps I should wait for more material.

My life had ended at age fourteen in the Silver Eagle tribe. In the present lifetime, I met Scott at age fourteen, and, as he did when he was my grandfather in that earlier lifetime, Silver Cloud, he advised me now: "It is time for you to let the book go, Janet, and get on with your healing work with people."

An incident occurred a few days later that helped me bring to a conclusion my account of the tribe. While I was cleaning out my files, discarding a multitude of the papers that seem to bury me from time to time, I came across a small five-by-seven inch paper from the Little Sioux, a mission in South Dakota. It was their response to Dot's inquiry about the words that had run through my mind during our first Medicine Wheel gathering in June of 1985 in Maryland. I had completely forgotten about that meditation experience. At the time I had felt the words were meaningless but Dot had written to the mission to ask if they could be translated.

Six years had passed. Now, as I unexpectedly came across the paper, I sat down, overwhelmed at the confirmation of my experience. The words I had heard in my meditation, although they were not written on the paper, freely returned to my mind: Ya-Na-Hene...Ya-Na-Hene....

I had never made a connection between that meditation experience and the lifetime about which I was now writing—the Silver Eagle tribe. Could those words actually have been the Oglala language that kept running through my mind? The language, as spoken at the time, no longer existed. The closest that could come would be the Lakota-Sioux.

I read the typewritten reply by Rev. Patrick McCorkell, the Director. He said that Father C. Jordan, to whom Dot had written for Lakota translations, says that in "stretching it" the meaning could be:

Now it can be said.

Is it true? Did the tribe exist? I don't know. All that I can do is share my story in the way that it actually happened in my life. Our memories have been strong. The experience of my own regression touched me in a way that I cannot explain except to say that *it touched my soul.* If we were, indeed, a tribe of "highly spiritual people attuned to the land and Great Spirit," it is also true of these people today—in this life. By bringing these memories back, we have been able to *free our spirits* from the pain of unconscious memories that held us back. We each have a deeper understanding of who we are—and that we are *so much more* than our physical bodies.

We were sincere with each other as the memories came. Could we have tapped into each other's unconscious minds and created a metaphor? Perhaps. Or—maybe—we are a tribe that has returned.

Then we had love, but no power.
Now we have love and power.
This time we will run over them with love.

—*Silver Eagle*

Notes

1. Third Eye—the sixth chakra. An area of psychic perception related to seeing/vision, located in the center of the forehead and connected to the pineal gland.
2. Months later I would remember the coincidence of Michael's mannerisms of speech: "My head says...but my heart says..."
3. Months later Karen would realize that she had been Native American.
4. After he came out of the hypnotic state, Scottie recognized his friend's name as Sitting Bear. Approximately three years after his regression Scottie remembered his own name to be Walks Tall.
5. Referring to Wildflower (Vicki Watkins).
6. On this trip we learned that Brian Cochrane and Dan had been Scottie's sons in the tribe. Jennifer Bower had been spirit energy that assisted us. During the Celebration, Scottie kept hearing the name "Claire, Claire." The only Claire that we knew was Ginger's guide. Again, Scottie was getting the name and asked Sara about it. She said that Claire was White Pine in the tribe, mate to Walks Tall (Scottie). When she saw him killed, White Pine rushed to be next.
7. About six months after my visit Dan saw a video by Pink Floyd depicting the music "Learning to Fly." "Mom, it blew me away," he said. "It's done in this time period, but there's a young boy on a high mountain and an old Indian appears."
8. According to Dr. Perestam, I had a weak subscapularis—the only muscle related to the heart—on both sides. My left fourth rib was subluxated and the fourth thoracic vertebrae was in a subluxated position, pushed and crowding my heart. The rib was pushed back and down, similar to a scissors affect on my heart. Both Pectoralis minor chest muscles were crowding the chest cavity. My heart was crowded to the right. A hiatal hernia was also affecting the heart position in a negative manner. [Dr. Perestam has given permission to use his name.]
9. This seems to correspond with Dan's memories of a young man going for help. ("I don't know if he made it.") As of this writing Dan and Heather have never met. Only after Heather's regression did I tell her

216

about Dan's memories, and only after Dan's trance work did I share Heather's regression with him.

10. Heather knew nothing about the baby (Elaine's) experience. She has never met Elaine.

11. Akasha is the stored record of everything that has happened.

12. Michael had never heard that Dan's Indian name was Flying Arrow. The feathers Michael referred to correspond to the wings of feathers that Dan wore, according to Dan's memory.

13. Spirit guide in this life.

14. Apparently this is what DeLaine saw—that they cut out my heart and gave it to Silver Eagle.

15. Before Roz knew that he had been a member of the tribe his painting showed a little girl searching for someone.

16. A set of messages that help to reach one's unconscious mind or High Self.

17. From *The Book of Runes* by Ralph Blum, St. Martin's Press, NY.